NETWORKING

The Art of Making Friends

Carole Stone

VERMILION
London

1 3 5 7 9 10 8 6 4 2

First published in the United Kingdom in 2001 by Vermilion, an imprint of Ebury Press, Random House, 20 Vauxhall Bridge Road, London SW1V 2SA www.randomhouse.co.uk

Random House Australia (Pty) Limited 20 Alfred Street, Milsons Point, Sydney, New South Wales 2061, Australia

Random House New Zealand Limited 18 Poland Road, Glenfield, Auckland 10, New Zealand

Random House South Africa (Pty) Limited Endulini, 5a Jubilee Road, Parktown 2193, South Africa

The Random House Group Limited Reg. No. 954009

Papers used by Vermilion are natural, recyclable products made from wood grown in sustainable forests.

Design and typesetting by Ferdinand Pageworks, London
Printed and bound in Great Britain by Cox & Wyman Ltd, Reading, Berkshire

A CIP catalogue record for this book is available from the British Library.

ISBN 0 09 185711 2

Contents

This book is dedicated to my mother, who gave me my interest in people, and to all the friends she encouraged me to make.

Prologue

Life handed me a big nose, small boobs, big feet and a rather coarse voice. On top of that I was painfully shy. But in the end – and to my surprise – none of this has prevented me from making friends and getting on with people.

These days I'm known as an extrovert networker – someone who not only knows lots of people but is always busy making the most of them. I think networking can make all the difference in your life – whether with your colleagues in the office, striking a business deal, starting a new job, or at home with young children. But for me the starting point for networking has always been my desire to make friends.

Making friends is an art – an art that can be learned. And once you've mastered this basic human skill you can go on to do whatever you want, in your personal life and at work, in a much more enjoyable and successful way.

Yet I'm astonished at how many of the people I meet, some extremely well-known and successful in their field, still feel at a loss when it comes to getting to know strangers – potential friends and useful contacts – whether at social occasions, work or business meetings. And when I wrote an article about 'small talk', I was overwhelmed by people wanting to hear more about 'breaking the ice', overcoming shyness and making friends.

As the future author of a book on making friends and networking, I was not promising raw material. Extremely shy in my teens and early twenties, I vividly remember standing outside the door of the office where I was a very junior secretary, in an agony of embarrassment, longing for someone else to come along so that I could slip in behind, unnoticed. In the lift at work I always stared at my shoes, too timid to look up and see who the stranger was standing next to me. But I've always found how other people live their lives fascinating, and in the end that has proved stronger than my shyness.

I have always loved the idea of connecting with other people – the essence of networking. But the confidence that I have today to approach people and make friends of them actually grew out of necessity.

I may have been shy when I was growing up, but my elder brother Roger was pathologically so – or so the doctors said. It was almost impossible to persuade him to talk to people outside our immediate family – my mother, my father and me. As a young child, and later as a teenager, Roger was difficult, often surly company, liable to throw a wobbly at any time. In his early twenties he was diagnosed as suffering from paranoid schizophrenia.

Roger's moods changed in a moment. He could be extremely aggressive and violent. He and my father (Dada had been a champion boxer in the regular Army) often came to blows – 'fisticuffs' as I preferred to think of them.

I think it was Roger's extreme shyness, his hostility towards other people and his utter inability to communicate when we were growing up that highlighted for me the tremendous importance of friendship. I wanted to include Roger in my friendships, but because of his behaviour people tended to give us a wide berth. I found I had to work really hard to make friends with people who would be prepared to put up with my brother's outbursts.

The effort I had to put in then is, I believe now, fundamental to the art of making friends. Friends are made, they don't just happen. You have to work at it.

Thumbing through my childhood autograph book recently, I came across an entry made when I was just eleven years old by Auntie Vi, my Godmother: 'The only way to have a friend is to be one', she wrote. That was sound advice.

Much more recently a long-standing friend gave me a book about the celebrated French writer Marcel Proust[1] (whom I've never yet got around to reading). The author, Alain de Botton, tells us that because Proust wanted so much to be liked he worked very hard at it. He ended up with legions of friends because he always made a point of asking them questions. Proust understood that most

[1] Alain de Botton; *How Proust Can Change Your Life*; Picador, 1997

people like to be asked about themselves; they find it flattering, and that's the way to make contact. It's all about recognising that other people are very similar to you. They want to be liked; they want to have friends – just as you do.

So I think the real art of making friends – of connecting with other people – is to take an interest in their lives as well as your own. If all you can ever think of is yourself and your own immediate needs, then friendship just won't happen.

These days I have over 14,000 names on my personal database, and a great many of them are much more than just contacts or even acquaintances – they've become friends. Some people think you can only have a handful of real friends – I don't see it like that. Of course some of my friends are closer than others, but as soon as I find I'm taking a real interest in someone I've met and wanting to see them again, I'm already thinking of them as a friend.

Friends are people you can help, and people who can help you – whether on a business or a personal level. They really are to me the essence of being human.

I've grown to love making new friends and introducing them to each other for the pure enjoyment I get out of it. And I earn my living putting together people from different worlds – business, politics and the media – who might otherwise never meet.

So this book has grown out of my personal and professional experience. I hope you'll draw from it the things that apply to your own life. It may give you the courage to pick up the phone and make that call to a friend you haven't spoken to for ages, to overcome your shyness in a business meeting and win over people important to your work, to start that conversation with a colleague who seems a bit distant, or just enjoy that social occasion that looks so intimidating.

It's your attitude to making friends and making the most of them that I hope my own experience can help you with, but there'll be plenty of practical hints and tips along the way.

In this book I'll be talking about how to go to parties with confidence and how to give them without worry; how to survive a snub and how to make successful small talk, how to network your friends and how to keep track of them all.

Some chapters deal with purely personal social occasions and others with business ones. At the end of each chapter I have highlighted what I call Friendly Behaviour – the things to remember as you set about meeting people and making friends. In the last chapter I have sketched out what can happen when you behave in a friendly or unfriendly way in various situations. And I leave you with Carole's Commitments, six principles which guide me as I go about making and networking my friends.

Learning the art of making friends has transformed my life. It's an added bonus that from time to time I feel that these connections really have 'made a difference' to other people's lives, as I think has sometimes been the case.

This book is all about making those connections: helping you make real contact with the people you meet, whether socially or at work. It's all about seizing the moment, taking every chance life offers you to make friends – and then making the most of them. The rewards are enormous.

1

People
we all need them

How does that wonderful Country & Western song go? 'A stranger is just a friend you haven't yet met'. I agree – I think of everyone I meet as a potential friend waiting to join my circle, and that's how *you've* got to look at it if you want to make more friends. Of course, not every one of those strangers will become a friend, but don't write them all off before you start.

The late Duchess of Windsor apparently said: 'You can't be too rich or too thin'. I'd say: 'You can't have too many friends.'

Making friends is easier than you think. They really are out there, but you have to go at least half way to meet them – because, like you, other people can be shy, uncertain and afraid of being rebuffed.

It you take that first step and extend the hand of friendship, it will, in most cases, be eagerly, if sometimes hesitantly, grasped in return. And what a wonderful feeling that is. One friend can lead to another and, if you want, you'll soon have a stock of friends, each having something different to offer – in the same way that you have different things to offer each of them.

I suspect lots of people don't realise how rewarding friends can be, and how we all need them to get through life's ups and downs with a chance of happiness.

Me, I had no real choice: despite my shyness I had to make friends somehow. Without them I would have found it far more difficult to cope with life.

My brother – the starting point

In Southampton, where we lived, my brother Roger had been banned from almost every pub in town: when he got cross he had a habit of throwing his beer over the person nearest to him. We had to tour the streets looking for somewhere that would let us in. And when we did gain entrance Roger would usually sit silent and angry, glaring at anyone who looked like making a friendly approach.

If Roger hadn't been so difficult, I might never have got to know someone who is now one of my oldest friends. I first met her at square dancing – you can see how hard I was trying to make friends, joining anything and everything, especially if I could get Roger to come along too. She was a girl of few words and a rather abrasive manner, who seemed as awkward as I felt. But we got to know each other because I persuaded her to join us for a cup of coffee in the shopping precinct at the weekend. She was unmoved by Roger's odd behaviour – there weren't many people like that – and treated him in a thoroughly matter of fact way. And, probably for that very reason, Roger was quite happy for her to be there. The more I met my new friend outside the square dancing sessions, the more I grew to appreciate her common sense approach to life. How glad I am that I needed to get to know her.

Recognising my need for friends, and understanding that I had to go out of my way to make them, was the start to overcoming my loneliness. In a way I feel it was Roger, despite all the problems his illness caused, who helped me develop that ability to make the friends that have made such a difference to my life. Sadly, Roger died from a stroke in his forties, but I think he would be pleased to know he'd got me started making friends.

Looks and brains aren't everything

At school I was never part of the 'in crowd': my big nose and small boobs probably didn't help – I've often wondered what it would have been like if it had been the other way round! I was what they called 'big boned': I knew they meant 'hefty'. But, as I eventually discovered, the fact is you don't have to be beautiful to make friends. If you're not, you sometimes try harder. And beauty can be off-putting. As a beautiful person you may have admirers, but friends may be harder to come by – particularly those of the same sex.

I was fairly quick to learn, but I didn't excel in exams. I was always in the B form: I never moved up to A. I worked hard for my eight 'O' levels, but didn't go on to university – instead I went to secretarial college to learn short-hand and typing. I'm certainly no egghead. But now, looking at the number of people I'm friends with today, I realise these things are irrelevant. Don't ever feel that a lack of staggeringly good looks or a great academic track record is a barrier to making good friends – it's not.

People who need people

I was very quiet at school and in my first secretarial job, but I found that shyness too can work in favour of friendship. Because I was always readier to listen than to talk about myself – however much I might have wanted to – I did begin to make the friends I craved. Then later at the BBC – where I would one day find myself running Radio 4's flagship discussion programme *Any Questions?* – my work forced me to go out and meet people. Again, because I really *did* want to hear what other people thought about things, what was important to them, I was a good listener. That helped me make friends too. And I got a great deal of help and comfort from what they had to say. I found solace in my friends, and I still do: I learn from them how they deal with what life throws at them – how they cope. And that helps me.

Gradually, I realised that if I tried hard enough to overcome my shyness I could make friends myself. I tried to put myself in the other person's place, to find out what was really on their mind, rather than just wondering what they thought of me. As I soon discovered, the sternest people melt when they think you could be interested in what they have to say.

It sounds as if I'm hooked on friends, and I suppose I am now an addict, a sort of compulsive friend-maker. I'm sure it stems from my early insecurity and doubt in my ability to manage my life without them. Barbra Streisand's line 'People who need people' could have been written for me.

You may be more self-sufficient than I am, but I think everyone can gain from meeting new people. And it's not a weakness but a strength to recognise that there are times when everybody needs a friend.

An old friend of mine was leaving her job as press officer for a national charity. Nearing retirement age, she was worried that she would no longer be taken seriously. I invited her to a business lunch where I knew she had something worthwhile to say. The following day I got a note from her to say how much it had meant to her – not just to meet the other people round the table, but to be introduced to them as someone who still counted. It had boosted her confidence. Already two of my guests had been in touch with her to discuss part-time work.

Another of my friends is a hugely successful career woman in her fifties who's always being invited to exciting places and meeting fascinating people. But recently her partner left her. What was it I asked her, that she missed most? It was, she said, that she no longer had this person to 'carry in her consciousness' throughout the day when they weren't together. She so missed those little moments when she used to see something that he would like, or think of something to tell him later, or just simply think of him and send a loving thought. She couldn't do that any more.

I've thought about that a lot since and I asked her later whether she felt the same way about close friends. She said she did and that, for her, this was the difference between acquaintances and friends. Friends, she says, are people we think about when we're not with them; we're conscious of caring about them, wondering how they're getting on. She mentioned someone we both knew who was going through a sad time and said she thought of this friend most days, sending her mental messages of support.

I don't disagree with that, but for me my friends, acquaintances and colleagues are all part of the same network of support. It's just that the strength of the ties that bind us together varies, depending on how long I've known them and how deeply I feel about them.

I remember reading an article by a woman journalist who'd had a long stay in hospital. She said that though many of her friends came to visit her she'd still felt lonely because she didn't have a partner of her own to come and see her. She looked enviously across the ward at other women patients as they were visited by their husbands or partners. But, as the days went by, she began to see that though she didn't have just one special visitor, she did have numerous friends who each gave her a different boost to help speed her recovery. She realised she'd been discounting the true value of those friendships. Now, as she thought about it, she mentally raised her friends to a higher level – and felt much better. She'd understood how essential friends can be.

There's an important point here. You never know when you're going to need those friends, and you can't always make friends instantly, just like that.

So make friends when you can. I didn't meet my future husband, the television journalist Richard Lindley, until I was in my forties. But in many ways I don't regret that. By then I'd built up a circle of trusted friends, and I knew I was never going to let go of them.

Friendly Behaviour

Friends are made – they don't just happen

Think of strangers as potential friends – take
that first step towards friendship

Be a good listener – find out what's on your
friend's mind

Don't worry that you're not good-looking or
clever – that's irrelevant in friendship

Carry your friends in your consciousness

Make friends when you can – you can't just
do it when you need help

Don't let your love for a partner make you
neglect friends – they're still important

2

Friends
the world is full of them

Not everyone has the same idea about the friends they'd like to make. Some will be delighted and content to make a friend of the person who lives over the road, or a colleague in the same office. Others may want to do that and more; they may be keen to meet people outside their usual circle. The great thing is that friendship need know no barriers; even the brightest of social stars will come out for you if you're nice to them.

I was once at a fund-raising event and spotted a well-known television comedian. I couldn't find the host to ask her to introduce me, and was a bit shy about barging into the admiring circle around him. So I waited until he looked free and then went straight over, holding out my hand and saying: 'I'm Carole Stone, I couldn't leave without saying hello to you, I love your television sketches'. He certainly didn't know who I was, but he looked pleased all the same. So I was encouraged to add: 'I'd love to invite you to my

Christmas party' (more about this later). I didn't ask him for his home address but later that year sent him an invitation through his agent. He came to my party, and my guests were as delighted as I was. So don't go away from a social occasion kicking yourself for not speaking to someone you'd love to have met. Give it a go.

In the same way, I was at a party following a West End premiere. Just as I was on the point of leaving, I spotted a young journalist I didn't know but had seen in a recent television programme. He was in the middle of a crowd, but I made myself go over, say who I was and tell him how good he'd been. I just couldn't resist making contact. A few days later I got a message from him saying how flattered he'd been that I'd enjoyed his appearance. I was pleased I'd made that extra effort and risked a possible rebuff. I know I'll invite him to my annual party this year and I'm now on the way to making another friend.

I was having supper with my husband Richard and a good friend I first met when she had just written a bestseller on dieting[2]. We were in a noisy little restaurant, tables all close together, in the seaside town of Whitstable in Kent, and about to order. I rather fancied what the man at the next table was eating, peered across at his plate and struck up a conversation with him. (Richard's quite used to this sort of thing, he knows I'm harmless!) We all started chatting. On leaving, being the compulsive friend-collector I am, I told this stranger I'd like to invite him and his wife to

[2] Audrey Eyton; *The F-Plan Diet*; Penguin, 1982

my Christmas party later in the year. He seemed pleased and at my request scribbled his name and address on a corner of his paper napkin. And I made sure he knew my name so that he could recognise it when my invitation arrived.

You've got to act swiftly if you're to take the chance of turning a stranger into a friend. They're lurking around unexpected corners; you just need to recognise their potential and put in a bit of effort to make sure you'll see them again. But how do we actually make these friends? How do we turn an acquaintance or a chance encounter into something more?

Taking action

It's a good idea always to have something up your sleeve, as I did that evening in Whitstable, to which you can invite someone – no matter how far in advance. I was helped by the fact that I already knew I would be holding my Christmas party, but it could have been any kind of social gathering, big or small, already sorted or yet to be planned.

For example, it could be a get-together that you hold regularly at your home – what I call my 'salon' (I'll be telling you more about that later). Or it could be a small gathering of some of your existing friends organised specially to introduce your new acquaintance. The fact is, you're unlikely to see this person, this potential friend, again unless you take some action. So be brave and make the first approach.

I was at a Party political conference a few years ago and wanted to meet a particular bright young policy maker. I just couldn't seem to track him down, until someone happened to mention his name and pointed him out to me. He was at the bar buying a round of drinks. I elbowed my way through the throng to his side, hoping to find an excuse to speak to him. In the crush he spilled his drinks all over me and apologised. I was charming, secretly delighted: 'Was he by any chance so and so?' He was. I gave him my card and asked if I could give him a ring to invite him to a lunch I was hosting. He said that was fine. I rang, he came, and we're now on friendly terms.

I'm not suggesting that you have to get a drink poured over you every time you want to make a friend, but the real point is this. When I did make contact with the person I wanted to meet I had something – in this case a lunch – up my sleeve to invite him to. Of course this was a work situation for me, but I still think it's a good idea, even in your private life, to have some social event planned to which you can invite someone you meet and decide is a possible friend.

Don't judge a book...

Making friends often means giving up preconceived ideas about people. You may think you don't want to make a friend of someone much younger or older than you, or someone in a line of work you're not interested in; but if you look again you could easily find that that person is not an alien creature but a new friend.

A girlfriend of mine always spends her holidays with a lady in her eighties – old enough to be her grandmother. At first I thought it odd, but when I saw the pleasure they gained from each other's company, the laughs they had and the travel they enjoyed, I thought again.

In the same way, I thought it was unlikely I would make friends with any of the high-profile people I met when I was producing BBC Radio 4's *Any Questions?* programme. But it turned out not to be true. For example, there was a lively woman barrister who's now become a member of the House of Lords. She was of course an expert on the law, which I knew very little about, and already very much one of the establishment. But I discovered that none of this mattered. We liked each other immediately and became firm friends: 'pals' as she puts it. Like many highly success-ful people I've since come to know, she turned out to be just as open to friendship as the rest of us.

Sometimes our very weaknesses can help us make friends. You'll find people are more than ready to respond if you reveal a little about your own shortcomings – the chances are they'll then tell you about theirs, and you've forged a common link.

I was at Heathrow airport, checking in for a holiday flight to America. I hate flying and my state of mind verges on desperation. Once seated I feel more and more anxious as I listen intently to every word of the safety patter; then I bury my head in a book during take-off and keep it there until I hear the welcome sound of the drinks trolley rattling down the aisle. On this particular occasion, I began chatting to the woman in front of me in the check-in queue and confessed my nervousness. It turned out that she too was a little apprehensive and was pleased when I suggested we ask for seats next to each other. In flight I ordered two stiff drinks and we agreed to meet again when back in England. I gave her my card – as ever, I'd made sure I had some cards handy before leaving home – and took a note of her telephone number. The important thing is that I said I would ring *her*. I did. We're still in touch. Do make sure you leave it that *you* will be the one to ring – then you can make certain that you do.

Another unusual occasion when I certainly hadn't expected to meet anybody was at a health farm I'd read about in a woman's magazine. It was in deepest Dorset, in southern England, and I intended to spend the weekend there without socialising. But this family-run holistic retreat was stricter than I'd expected. No television or radio was allowed and nothing whatsoever was to be eaten between the extremely spartan meals. By the Saturday teatime I'd had enough of herb tea and small portions and was absolutely starving. I sneaked quietly down to the kitchen (out of bounds) to hunt for any sign of food. I made straight for the bread tin, but another resident was there before me – with the same thing in mind. We both jumped guiltily, then dissolved into giggles, grabbed the loaf and ran. We left the health spa not much slimmer, but the best of friends. I hadn't gone there to make friends, but was open enough to the opportunity when it bumped into me.

Seizing the chance

You may think you have no opportunity to meet new people, but if you really want to you can create those opportunities. For example, when new neighbours move into your area, call round or drop a note of welcome through their letterbox. I did this with the man who moved into the penthouse above my flat. He turned out to be a major player in the media business that is my world. He's now both a useful contact and a friend.

When your child tells you there's a newcomer in class, keep a lookout for the new mum and make contact. These friendly gestures can often lead to new friendships.

Scour the local papers for groups and talks you think will interest you, or join the committee of your child's school, or the local residents' group. I joined the Covent Garden Community Association when I first moved into my London flat. I made myself take the time to attend committee meetings and deliver newsletters. In return, I got to know several of the members and learned a lot about the local area. Having made those friends helped make me feel I belonged in my new surroundings.

I also joined the Friends of St Martin-in-the-Fields in London's Trafalgar Square, which is the church where I worship. I often attend Choral Evensong on Sunday evening and stay for a cup of coffee after the service. It's a good place to meet people who've all come together for the same purpose. Having a shared interest is a great way to start conversations and make new friends. Take the lead: take things a stage further by proposing you buy a drink of some sort at the end of a meeting.

Most people want to meet new people but are hesitant to make that first move – so make sure it's you who does. For instance, I've made the chore of turning out my cupboards more enjoyable by joining forces with a friend. We took what we both wanted to throw out to a car boot sale. It was good fun; we bought ourselves lunch (and developed our friendship) with some of the proceeds.

Whatever you do, don't mope at home wishing you had somewhere to go and someone to go with. Sit by the phone by all means – not waiting for it to ring, but with your address book in your lap. Call to invite someone round – or arrange to meet them for a snack locally. It needn't cost a lot. And even if you're unsuccessful, at least you've reminded people you're about: next time they may ring you.

Don't give up just because someone is unresponsive to your first attempt at friendship. Try to find a shared interest, and if there's something going on in your area that's relevant, invite your potential friend to come along as your guest.

Making friends is a continuing business, whatever your age or situation in life. There are always people out there who'd be glad of a chance to get to know you and enrich your life. I think if someone had said that to me at school or secretarial college I would have found it hard to believe. When you're shy and socially awkward it's difficult to imagine that anyone else can feel the same, that they can be just as insecure inside as you are. You may feel that they can't have any need of you or your friendship. I think they do.

I know a high-powered American business woman, who has been appointed the Managing Director of an investment bank. She's to be based in New York at some vast salary. I met her at a supper party and assumed she'd be far too busy to accept any invitation from me. Nevertheless I invited her to a business lunch and she came. A little later I asked her to my flat for lunch and again she said 'yes'. She's now a good friend, so much so that she came to my wedding. Now I'm planning to help her start her own 'salon' in New York. That'll be a whole new country for me to explore in my search for friends!

The lesson is this: don't think the person you meet is bound to be too busy, too rich or too important to have time for you. When you're reluctant to make contact with someone you feel doesn't need your friendship, give it a go anyway. That person may turn out to be really pleased to hear from you.

Friendly Behaviour

Act swiftly – seize the chance to
make a friend

Aim to have a social event planned to offer
to potential friends

Be ready to find friends outside your
usual circle

Keep your contact details with you ready
to hand out

Admit your own shortcomings – others
may respond

Look out for newcomers to your area – and
welcome them

Find local groups where you can meet
new people

Don't rule out busy or important people –
they need friends too

3

Personal Best
What to expect from friends

I have a girlfriend I talk to on the phone at least every other day, about nothing very much: mostly just light, inconsequential chatter. We met when we were both in the WRNR (Women's Royal Naval Reserve) and we've known each other now for over 30 years. We're both tall, nearly 5' 10", and both have big feet, size 10. We first made contact waiting on the edge of the parade ground for our extra-large Navy issue shoes to arrive so that we could take part in the drill. I think you could say it was being tall – coupled with the desperate search to find a man – that kept us together. But as friends today we still fulfil a real need in each other.

Once, when I'd been away on holiday for a few weeks, my friend told me how much she'd missed me 'rabbitting on'. I understood exactly what she meant, and I wasn't offended. We have a sort of friendly short-hand: she'll drone on endlessly about a hopeless boyfriend, who in my view never treats her well enough; I mutter the odd word of sympathy and assent at pregnant pauses. Then it's my turn to witter on: about how I work too hard, eat too much and how yet again I'm definitely starting my diet on Monday. It works. Mostly we don't explore the depths in our souls when we speak, but we each know what we expect from our friendship and we're very fond of each other.

So don't feel that every friendship has to be intense – there's a great deal to be said for friends who are a comfort rather than a source of drama. We're talking about friendship, not a passionate affair.

And don't expect more from your friends than they have the ability to give. I recently heard an Olympic champion talking about her fellow athletes on the radio. She referred to their 'P.B.' – their Personal Best. I think that's the most any of us can expect from our friends.

Keeping your perspective

I need to remember this whenever I make a new friend. I have a habit of going completely overboard when I first meet someone: they're 'utterly delightful, witty, generous, warm'. I invite them everywhere. Then, when they inevitably show signs of being a little less than perfect, I am not only unreasonably disappointed – I am cross.

That was just what happened when I met a bright young entrepreneur through a mutual friend. He was just back from abroad and rather out of touch. He wanted me to include him in my network. I was pleased to invite him to one or two of my business lunches to get him back in circulation. In return he offered to organise a lunch for me so that I could meet some of his colleagues in marketing. I thought it was a very nice gesture. But in the event he merely threw half a dozen names and telephone numbers in my direction and left me to approach these people 'cold'. I found myself arranging – and paying for – the whole thing. I was cross, and so disappointed that my friend was not quite as wonderful as I had imagined him to be. My mistake.

I now keep my initial enthusiasm in check: these days I prefer to discover an unexpected extra quality in a new-found friend, rather than rushing in expecting them to be perfect.

But my new friend also got it wrong. What he should have done, at the very least, is to have rung the people he was suggesting I meet to say I'd be making contact. That would have made it so much easier for me. And he should have followed through with his offer to arrange the lunch and done exactly that. I've forgiven him now but, as you'll find me saying all through this book, if you make an offer to do something, you must deliver on your promise.

Friendship is a two-way deal – the more you are pre-pared to give and share, the more you can expect from the friendship in return. What you give to your friends can be many things – the generosity of sharing contacts and other friends; your company; advice and your emotional support. And the more you open up about your own failings, hopes, fears, even tragedies, the closer the friendship can become.

The beauty of friends is that each of them offers you something different, and it's not always what you would expect.

One Christmas a good friend of mine, a radio and television presenter, invited me and my family to join her and a group of her friends for Boxing Day lunch. She made a point of including my brother Roger, although she was well aware that he suffered from schizophrenia. His behaviour was always unpredictable. As it was, Roger was pleased to be asked and behaved well. And my friend did more than invite him, she went out of her way to make him feel welcome. That was a friend in action. I won't forget that little act of kindness.

I have a friend I made quite recently, who is an author. She's a bit younger than me, a strong feminist and far more of an 'issues' person than I am. Yet surprisingly, I find I can talk to her about my feelings more easily than I can to some of my more long-standing friends who are the same age as me.

Friends as family

I was very moved the other day when the friend I met so long ago in the WRNR rang me. She was about to go into hospital for an operation on her knee. Because she has no relatives living in this country she asked if she could give my name as her 'next of kin'. I really felt like family.

The sociologist Professor Ray Pahl[3] writes about the changing nature of friendship. In many cases, he says, friends are replacing the family. I agree. Because families are breaking up more often and because relatives now frequently live far away, no longer in the next street, friends have become more important.

For me, Professor Pahl's research demonstrates what I've always instinctively felt – that friendships are vital. They can provide crucial support when families are far apart. And for all of us, friends can help us pick up the pieces when relationships fail, or comfort us when we find ourselves alone without any family.

Today it is our friends who define us as the people we are. Instead of looking at our family background or where we come from, others weighing us up look at our friends – the company we keep – to help them work out the sort of people we are. More than family, it is now the people we *do* things with that matters. And unlike family, friends are a matter of choice; there are no limits, no boundaries to friendship.

In a crisis it can be easier to turn to a friend than to a family member, who may bring with them a shared burden of emotional baggage from the past. I have a friend whose only child tragically committed suicide in his mid-twenties. My friend says she was utterly relieved that her

3 Ray Pahl; *On Friendship*; Polity, 2000

mother was already dead and that she didn't have to turn to her and bear her sorrow as well as her own. From the moment she rang to tell me the terrible news that she had just found her son dead, I phoned her every day for a year – she lives a long way from London – just trying to help as a friend. I know she would do the same for me. We will I think remain friends for life. She has always shown herself a friend to me in so many different ways – often just by listening to me and giving me her wise advice. She's always encouraged me in all my new ventures – such as this book.

And when I have good news to tell her she really is thrilled to hear it. That's rare. The American writer Gore Vidal says: 'Whenever a friend succeeds a little something inside me dies'. I suspect there's an inkling of truth in that for most of us, but real friendship rises above it.

Professor Pahl suggests that as well as friends becoming more like families, today's families are becoming more like friends.

I certainly considered my mother my best friend. I could discuss anything with Mama and never found her an emotional burden. She gave me clear advice, uncluttered by sentimentality, and that advice encouraged me to widen my circle outside the family by making friends. She loved to see the warmth and support they brought in addition to what she could offer me.

In the same way I also think of Eileen, my mother's sister and only ten years older than me, as more of a close and valued friend than an aunt. We speak on the phone two or three times a week. Eileen is always prepared to listen to what I have to say. She doesn't pontificate, and whatever advice she does give she practises herself. Eileen has had to face up to a great deal in her life, and the straight-forward courage she's shown has always been an example to me.

Nobody's perfect

I don't want to suggest that friends are the perfect remedy for all the pains and problems in your life – or always a better alternative to the family. However important, friends are not infallible: they can disappoint, and, as I've already said, make you very cross at times. On these occasions, I find it helps to write down the things about them that are annoying me, then tick off those I'm prepared to forget. If something still niggles away, I ring the friend and face it head-on.

I try not to let resentment fester, if I feel a friend has let me down in some way, just because I had expected better behaviour. I've found it's worth stepping back and taking stock of the situation. Try to imagine how the other person is feeling: it could be that they are unsure, out of their depth, looking for a way to resolve the differences between you. And you must be prepared to wipe the slate clean every now and then.

Accept that some of your friends' traits will always irritate you. You just need to feel that their good points outweigh their faults.

The same applies in the work situation. In my own small office in my flat I have a part-time assistant-cum-secretary on whom I rely to see that all the arrangements for meetings and lunches are clearly known to everybody involved in good time. There are CV's to be faxed, details of the venue to be up-dated and messages to be passed on. It's absolutely vital for my professional reputation that all this happens perfectly. When it doesn't, and my assistant forgets to confirm some arrangement or leaves sending a fax too late, I feel terribly let down. I ask for an explanation immediately and we have it out there and then. After that we're fine. And I remind myself of why I'm so pleased to have that assistant around. Her way of dealing with my friends and business contacts when they ring, her ability to trouble-shoot when the phones go down or the computers pack up, and above all her total loyalty and good humour – all these qualities more than compensate for the occasional lapse.

What you can't change, accept – if you want to keep your friendship. I have a friend who just can't stop himself telling me the same anecdotes again and again. I've tried everything, from listening intently to every word, to interrupting him with the punch line, all to no avail. But I've decided I want to remain friends with him and now I just let the words wash over me.

You may even have to recognise that some friends are '24s' – that means you can't be in their company and remain on good terms for longer than 24 hours at a time. I find this is the case with one of my out-of-town friends who just has to be the centre of attention. So I limit her visits to 24 hours, and find I can devote that time to her without wanting to scream or hit her over the head. Never go on holiday with friends you know in your heart are really '24s'!

Don't let unnecessary problems come between you to spoil a friendship. I spent my teens reading the romantic novels published by Mills & Boon or written by Georgette Heyer. You know the stories ('heart be still!') where the hero and heroine don't tell each other what's really on their mind until the last chapter; you have to agonise through page after page of misunderstandings. Don't let this happen in real life. It's so unnecessary and can with a bit of thought be avoided. If there's something you don't understand about your friend's behaviour take it up with them straightaway, and preserve your friendship.

Whatever you do, don't allow friendships to peter out because neither of you has tried to resolve an argument. Some friends will find it too hard to make that first move – so let it be you. Don't be proud or prickly – just pick up the phone and say you're sorry not to have seen your friend recently and suggest you meet. Of course there's a chance you'll be rebuffed, but I've found that on the whole friends want to make up.

Richard and I invited one of his old journalist friends to a dinner party. On the night, when he hadn't turned up, we gave him a call, only to find he'd completely forgotten about the dinner. But he grabbed a taxi, arrived in time for the main course and stayed until the early hours of the morning. Then we heard nothing from him whatsoever – not even a telephone call. Richard would have let the friendship drop. But I knew they'd known each other for years and a few months later I invited him to a drinks party. He came, and rather sheepishly apologised for not having been in touch, saying he'd left it so long he'd felt too embarrassed to ring or write. He was obviously glad of the opportunity my invitation had given him to restore the friendship.

It's fine for a friend to dump a heavy load of problems on you, perhaps because of a collapsing relationship or an unexpected bereavement; but on the whole I think it's fair to expect friendship to be a two-way traffic – otherwise you're not a friend but a therapist. If this off-loading goes on and on, and you find you're left permanently exhausted with your friend's angst (it may be off their chest, but now it's on yours), then you must say so.

I know I've been guilty of this. You usually off-load your worries on the person you are seeing most of at the time – for me it used to be my BBC colleagues who had to put up with my agonising over boyfriends. It was ages before I reminded myself this was not the way to behave – either for my work or my friendships.

The experts tells us that those with close and supportive friends are happier and healthier. But bear in mind that wonderful line at the end of *Some Like it Hot*. Jack Lemmon, disguised as 'Daphne' has become engaged. When he finally pulls off his wig to reveal that he's really a man his 'fiancé' replies: 'Nobody's perfect!' That's right. Rather than demand that everyone you know be the perfect friend, complete in every way, value each of your friends for their different qualities – just as each of them gets something different from you. That way you make the most of friends, and discover what a central part of life they really are.

Friendly Behaviour

Remember that each friendship offers
something different

Friendships can be deeply rewarding
without being deeply dramatic

Friends can sometimes help where family
members can't

If you're cross with a friend, sort it out –
don't let it ruin your friendship

Friendship is a two-way relationship – you're
a friend, not a therapist

In the office deal with your colleagues'
lapses – and value their strengths

Accept your friends for what they are –
nobody's perfect

4

Party, Party
going and giving

I'm known as a party giver; people assume that I delight both in giving parties and in going to them. And it's true that mostly I do. I certainly never turn down an invitation because it sounds intimidating, but even after years of pretty successful networking I can still find myself very nervous indeed when I'm invited out.

For all but the most self-confident, entering a room full of people who seem to know each other better than you do is a very intimidating experience. 'Why will anyone want to talk to me?', I ask myself. Perhaps that's what you feel too.

Keep smiling through

You know how it is when you're introduced to someone at a social occasion and then left to fend for yourself. You can almost feel the other person sense your fear and clam up in front of you. How should you react? It's hard not to go equally rigid, but you could try giving a smile instead and saying: 'I don't know another soul here, I'm so glad to be able to chat to you for a moment.' At the very least it will get you through the next few minutes; at best it could be the start of a friendship that lasts the rest of your life.

Try to look upon every social occasion not as a looming nightmare that you must somehow survive, but rather as an opportunity to meet a new friend. And it's important to smile and keep smiling.

That's something I learned back in the early 60's when I signed up for two evenings a week at the Lucy Clayton Charm School. I came to London for the course and worked as a temp in the daytime to pay for it. I stayed with relatives. I'd signed up because I wanted to be a journalist and I wasn't sure I knew how to turn myself out or how to behave with other people. It was the first time I had met the seriously rich – the course was full of debs. They were incredibly sweet to me, the girl from the sticks with no make-up, no evening dresses and no knowledge of the world. That's when I realised that I could make friends with people who were very different from me. I was so proud when I got the highest marks at the end of the course – even though I later learned we were marked on how much we'd improved. I'd obviously started at rock bottom!

For me the essence of Lucy Clayton's Charm Course was to keep smiling in any social situation, no matter how intimidating it seems to be. And I was glad of that training when I went to a party in a new friend's home in a fashionable part of London. The host was a very amiable and successful journalist I'd run into a few times at media meetings, but his wife I scarcely knew. As I arrived I could hear the loud noise of conversation coming from the first-floor window of their house – this was the 'chattering classes' in action. I felt rather intimidated as I rang the bell. The door was opened by one of the other guests who shouted: 'drinks upstairs!' before he shot off in a different direction. As I was climbing up I saw my hostess below. She waved a welcome, but then disappeared into the kitchen. The party room was humming, everyone deep in what sounded like very clever discussion, all looking extremely smart in a casual sort of way. I made my way politely past three or four groups of people without anybody paying me any attention. Eventually I saw someone I knew and edged my way over. He vaguely introduced me to the people he was talking to and then rushed off to chat to someone else. My group resumed their conversation without including me. I was left wondering if I could escape the party unnoticed, but quickly dismissed the thought – I just couldn't allow myself to admit defeat and leave. I was wishing I'd managed to persuade Richard to come with me. The trouble is he is just not as social as I am and shamelessly cherry-picks only the invitations he wants to accept – leaving me to fend for myself at the rest.

There was nothing for it but to give it a go.

I took a deep breath and firmly introduced myself to the man standing nearest to me, asking how he knew our host. Apparently they worked together on the same newspaper. He then in turn introduced me to the rather gloomy looking man he'd been talking to and went off to find me a drink. Their previous conversation had been incomprehensible to me – shoptalk about the inner workings of their paper, so I didn't feel able to continue that topic. Worse, I hadn't had a chance to read any newspaper at all that day. The best I could manage, since there was a fuel crisis at the time, was to ask the stranger rather lamely how he'd managed to get to the party, by car or public transport. Fortunately at that point someone I knew joined us, my glass of wine arrived and I began to relax.

I left about an hour later, having struck up a conversation and exchanged telephone numbers with a couple of people I wanted to see again. So it was worth it in the end. If Richard had been there it would have been much easier at the beginning, but after about half-an-hour he would have been wanting to go. What's more, he prefers that we stick together at a party, which makes it less likely I'll meet new people. So in spite of everything I'm glad I went on my own, and kept my nerve.

Be prepared

So many simple things would have made that party much easier for me: for example, if one of my hosts had been at the door to greet me, or get me safely started in conversation.

But I was more to blame. If only I'd been sensible enough to prepare myself in a small way by reading the papers before going somewhere I knew perfectly well was going to be full of high-powered journalists. When a social occasion like that is on the horizon, you do need to think about it beforehand if you feel you might be tongue-tied. Try to brief yourself on what's in the news for topics of conversation. You don't have to make yourself an expert, but if you know people from a particular profession will be there, have some suitable questions in your mind. I should have taken the trouble to do it; it would have made my first ten minutes there less of an ordeal.

When to join a group and how long to stay before you leave it is always a difficult judgement. It's a matter of being alert to other people and aware of their reactions. If you sense two people are desperate to talk on their own about something, you can just politely say you have to re-fill your glass and move off. If you're in a group but running out of conversation, then make your excuses and leave: 'I must have a word with so and so before they go', for example. But never leave anyone standing on their own – bring someone else into the conversation and introduce them to each other before you slip away.

Forgetting someone's name is always embarrassing. Try introducing them to a friend whose name you do remember, saying: 'This is Veronica Smith'. With any luck, the guest whose name you've forgotten will introduce themselves. Otherwise, just be honest and say something like: 'I remember your face, but I just can't remember your name'. Most people won't mind at all.

These days, as well as going to a lot of functions, I do a lot of entertaining myself. So I'm now acutely conscious of what it takes to create the right atmosphere for people to meet and make friends. But I didn't know much about all this on the day I held my own very first party, one Sunday lunch time long ago in Bristol, where I was working as a radio producer at the BBC. 'Will anyone turn up?', was all I could think about.

My first party

When I was growing up we never had any sort of knees-up or social get-together at home: my uncle Bob and cousin Margaret came to stay for the holidays, but that was about it. My parents were running a small sweet and tobacco shop with very long opening hours and my father also had a milk round to bring in a bit of extra money. We never thought of asking anyone to the house. My father would usually sit in his armchair in the evening with the *Psychic News*, reading out loud to us stories of weird happenings, and telling us five million readers couldn't be wrong. Any entertaining that went on was down at the pub. I progressed from waiting outside with a pineapple juice and a pickled egg, to being allowed into the bar for a lemonade shandy and bag of potato crisps – and, if I was lucky, a go on the one-armed bandit. We might have bought a round of drinks at the pub, but we never entertained at home.

Now all that was to change. For the first time ever I was going to give it a go as hostess in my cosy little Bristol flat.

The living room of my flat was just big enough to seat a dozen and I thought that if necessary one or two could sit on the floor. I'd borrowed some extra plates and cutlery from the staff canteen at work and some glasses from the off-licence. For help, I turned to a good friend now living in London. She brought two home-made trifles with her, made sure my flat looked respectable, and went shopping with me for lots of cheese and crusty bread. Another of my guests – we'd met at the Junior Chamber of Commerce – helped me choose the wine: something inexpensive, but definitely drinkable. (I'm delighted to say that I was able to repay him a few years later by introducing him to a girl-friend of mine, with whom he is now very happily settled.)

I was expecting about a dozen people including four from the BBC. I'd also plucked up courage to invite a well-known writer and agony aunt whom I'd met when she took part in a *Woman's Hour* programme produced in Bristol a few months earlier. I'm tempted to say she was my star guest, but I've learned not to treat any of my guests as a star, even if they are. If you do, you're in danger of giving them too much attention and making them uncomfortable – quite apart from annoying your other guests. Nevertheless, I was delighted she'd been able to accept.

She later met my mother and was very generous with practical advice on how to seek help for my brother Roger's illness. I think the urge I have to put people together stems from my early feelings that if only I could introduce Mama to the right people I could in some way lighten her load and make her life happier.

Among the other guests was a hot-air balloonist and his wife, who brought two of the home-made lemon tarts she knew I loved. Then there was the woman who lived round the corner. I often used to meet her walking her dog. Dogs by the way can be of great help in meeting potential friends – they introduce human beings to each other beautifully. I'd also included my former flatmate, a beautician, and her partner.

I'd sent them all invitations, which I'd typed out and then run off on the copier at work. I'd asked people to come '12.30pm for 1pm – drinks and buffet lunch'.

Several people I'd invited had turned me down – other things already planned, they said – and one couple hadn't replied. I should have checked they'd received the invitation, but hadn't the courage to in case they had, but just couldn't be bothered to reply. I found out later that they'd been away. These days I do always check if I've had no reply, and it's proved a sound move – it's always possible that your invitation simply didn't arrive.

These days I'm more worried that people will arrive too early rather than too late, but as the minutes ticked on past 12.30pm that Sunday lunch time, I began to think that no-one would come at all. Then at 12.40pm my first guests crossed the threshold – my spirits soared. A few minutes later another couple arrived and we were away…

I made sure everyone's glass was full and started to relax. I was a hostess in my own home, and I loved it. I still do. To give enjoyment to your friends and acquaintances can be an exciting and satisfying experience.

A party is a wonderful way to keep in touch with old friends and to make new ones. You can be bold as you like and make the mix of guests as wide as you wish. It can be centred around an anniversary or new home, or you can just decide it's time to bring everyone together.

I confess that I've never been interested in what kind of food I offer – though I love eating it – only in the people I'm inviting. I think some shy people may actually try and hide behind all the lovely eats they've prepared. They think, 'Well, I've done all that, surely my guests will be happy. I don't need to do any more'. People certainly like to feel you've made an effort for them, but food alone is not what makes a party a success. Nor are the surroundings. Don't ever worry that your home is not smart or that you can't afford a big spread. It really isn't the classy cutlery or elaborate dishes that make a party a hit. Successful entertaining is all about people: the mix of guests – that what's vital. More about this later.

I so enjoyed that first party I gave in Bristol that I soon found myself entertaining two or three times a year. I was, and still am, staggered at how the most unlikely people find they have some personal or business interest, or a friend, in common. Gradually, and mostly through this simple entertaining, I started to make more and more friends.

I began holding a Christmas drinks party on a weekday December evening. The numbers grew until I could no longer pack everyone into my home. Instead I hired the cellar in a local wine bar.

My Christmas party

The inspiration for my Christmas party was my darling mother (she died in her mid-seventies). I wanted her to have the chance of meeting more of my friends and colleagues. And I wanted them to have the pleasure of meeting her. The party started in Bristol. Then when I moved to London, still with the BBC, my party went with me. By now, all idea of food had gone completely out of the window; it was just drinks – wine, orange juice and mineral water.

I held the London party at the club I'd joined there – the Reform Club in Pall Mall. But be warned: the moment you start entertaining outside your home there can be problems. The Reform Club had a strict dress code – no jeans, and men must wear jacket and tie.

I remember that a rather flamboyant artist, who'd just arrived at Heathrow on his way back to his home in Cornwall, made a special effort to come to my party. He was wearing a colourful cravat. Because he didn't want to change it for the tie he was offered, he was refused entry to the Club. And so were several others who arrived in jeans. I didn't realise what had happened until after the party, and had to ring my disappointed guests to apologise. I learned the hard way that if there is a dress code your invitation must mention it.

When I first entertained in the Reform Club's Library, I was limited to a maximum of 250 guests because of fire regulations. I wasn't the least bit worried – that number

49

seemed way beyond my ambition; only 120 people came to that first Reform Club event and I had to ask for screens at either end of the room to stop it looking empty.

Ten years later, 650 people climbed the elegant staircase to my Christmas party, and the Library couldn't hold them all. There was a terrible squash. A lady had a seizure – she collapsed and passed out on the floor right next to the then Health Minister. Saying he was a politician not a doctor, he quickly made way for another of my guests who was medically qualified. Meanwhile the political editor of a tabloid newspaper had appeared on the scene. His wife overheard a senior journalist from a more upmarket paper suggesting that her husband was just looking for a sleazy story rather than trying to help. An altercation followed and a glass of wine was thrown – with the glass. Later a journalist was observed mopping a drop or two of blood from his brow in the gent's lavatory.

The Reform Club decided that my overcrowded party was all too much for their fire regulations, their floorboards – and their dignity. Politely, I was asked to find another venue; somewhere bigger, somewhere else …

I did, and now I welcome over a thousand guests to my annual Christmas party. But despite the numbers, I've tried to hang on to what I think makes a party work. For me, as ever, it's personal contact. I try to greet all my guests as they arrive – it's just a quick handshake or peck on the cheek, but at least we 'clock' each other. I know I'm reaching the limit to the number of friends I can invite and still welcome personally because these days there's a queue of people waiting to say 'hello'. In fact I got a note from one guest last year saying he enjoyed the queue ('wonderful conversation') – but was sorry he couldn't stay for the party. That's something I must certainly avoid happening in future.

Unusually for me I'm less willing to go to parties myself in those weeks leading up to my own. It's because I feel awkward when I come across people I have invited to my party before, but haven't had room for this year. And if any of them asks if I'm holding my party again this year, I feel compelled to send them an invitation as soon as I get home. Even if my party is mentioned in front of someone else I only know slightly, I feel I should invite them too!

But I love sending out the invitations. I look forward to seeing my old friends, plus new friends and business colleagues who haven't yet been to one of my parties. And then there are people I've met during the past year who I hope will become my friends too. It gives me such pleasure to think of all these different people mingling with each other at my party. My parties remain a matter of personal invitation. No matter how large they have become, it's certainly not open house. I agonise over every potential guest, longing to invite new friends but reluctant to lose anyone from the past. An old friend complains that every November I suffer from PPT – Pre-Party Tension. So these days, with space at such a premium, I don't encourage people to bring a friend or partner unless I know them well too. All the same if they ring and ask if they can do so, I tend to say 'yes'. And I think this is the best way to respond, otherwise you risk losing old friends – and you may miss out on a new one. And anyway, I often ask people who are inviting me somewhere if I can bring my partner.

Now that the party has become a regular annual event, I sometimes receive telephone calls a week or two before the date from people wanting to remind me of their existence, I suspect in the hope of an invitation. And of course, because I still feel thrilled and flattered that people want to join me at my party and be my friend, I invite them. They say it takes one to know one, and it's just the sort of thing I do myself. I recently left a timely message on the voice mail of a friend of mine who'd just got married. I'd heard they were holding a celebration reception very soon, but so far I hadn't been asked. I was absolutely thrilled when an invitation arrived later that week – after my phone call. I can't be sure that my call made the difference or what my girlfriend thought about it, but when it happens to me, the fact is I don't mind at all.

At my Christmas party I welcome my family and friends. There are people in the media, politicians and business people I work with, and people I see all the time, such as our newsagent, the couple who run the local dry cleaners and my hairdresser. The greatest compliment for me is to hear that my party still has a 'family' atmosphere and warmth. Perhaps friendship really is taking over some of the close connections the best kind of families used to offer.

Because it's grown so big, my Christmas party now costs me a fortune – but I think it's worth it. There have been times when I've spent my money on the party, rather than take my annual holiday, but I don't care!

Creating a great party

It's you and the people you invite who together make any party a success. So the guest list is your first priority. Whatever the size of your party, be bold. By all means invite people who you think will have similar interests, but don't worry about it. When your guests have to work a bit harder to find out about someone, rather than just talk 'shop', they'll learn so much more about them. As I've said, people constantly tell me as they're leaving that they've found something in common with another of my guests – something I could never have anticipated.

So experiment with the mix of guests: don't hold back from inviting people from as many different worlds and age groups as you can. So often people rarely meet those outside their own set – you can make this happen.

Next, send out your invitations in good time – between two and three weeks in advance is best. I have my Christmas party invitation run off at the local copying shop. I don't spend a lot of money on it: it's on pink card and has been rudely described as looking like a flyer for a car boot sale. The RSVP on the bottom of the invitation is important. I make sure I give my postal and email address, telephone and fax numbers. And if your venue is hard to find, do include a little map with the invitation, and perhaps a note about car parking.

However big or small the party, put the start and finish time on the invitation. That way guests can plan their day, and everybody knows when you are going to stop serving food and drink. Never ever hold a party that lasts all day, or even longer than a couple of hours. If you do, everyone will end up 'tired and emotional', and your guests could easily miss the people you really wanted them to meet.

When you've had some positive replies, you can afford to experiment by asking more people – perhaps those you know slightly but would like to know better. People always drop out on the day so you can take the risk of inviting more than you can really handle. You can mention the party to friends and colleagues you happen to come across, or you can just make a call to people at the last minute on the off chance that they're free to join you. I love these last minute invitations myself and I don't think most people are in any way offended by them. Make it easy for people to leave their attendance at a party open to the last minute if they wish. If you push too hard for a definite yes or no you could lose them. It's usually only a matter of having a few extra glasses and perhaps a bit more food on hand in case they do ring at the last minute to say that they can, after all, join you.

If it's more than just drinks and you're holding a 'fork' lunch or supper party, have the list of those who've accepted handy and tick them off as they arrive. And as soon as everyone's there you can serve the food. If someone is very late, just go ahead and make a start anyway.

Make a note of anyone who doesn't turn up – give them a ring there and then if you can. Otherwise contact them the next day to find out what happened. Also, make a note of people who couldn't accept your invitation this time but whom you've promised you'll invite on a future occasion. Don't just let them 'fall through the slats', as Richard sometimes urges me to do.

Don't be upset or offended if there is a big drop-out rate from your guest list. I always allow for it, even among those who have accepted my invitation, especially at Christmas time. People intend to be with you, but things can crop up at the last minute – a sudden business trip for example. By the way, if you want to remain someone's friend, do always let them know in advance, however near the date, if after all you're not going to be able to make it. And if you fail to do that, you must, must, ring afterwards and apologise for not being there.

Once the guests have arrived and the party is in full swing, it's time to concentrate on your role as host. Even at the smallest party the host or hostess must expect to be on the go continually. It's exhilarating – and exhausting. For me it's not enough to greet your guests at the door and leave them to it. I try to separate partners, take one to one group and one to another and introduce people to each other with what I hope is a helpful one-liner: 'This is Patsy, I think her children go to the same school as yours'; 'Bob, I want you to meet Jane, she's in advertising like you'.

If there are two of you hosting the party, one can make sure the glasses are filled while the other answers the door and keeps the guests circulating. If you're on your own, recruit a guest who will look after the drinks for you. Shy people often feel better, and find it easier to chat, if they have something specific to do, a role to play.

Nobody would ever get a drink at my Christmas party

if I didn't have waiters to serve it – it's just too big these days – but at any party in my home I try to avoid hired staff, because I think it can spoil the informal atmosphere. I'd rather keep everything simple and do as much as I can myself or get Richard and maybe a few friends to deal with coats and pour drinks.

If there is buffet food make sure you move your guests around between platefuls. This applies whether they're sitting down or standing. There's always a further opportunity to move people again over coffee. But if you take someone away from one group to join another, always bring someone else back so that the first group doesn't feel abandoned. Then it's time for you to move on again yourself.

Now this is entirely up to you, but I find I have the urge to clap my hands at some point early on in the party and just say very simply: 'Welcome, I'm so glad you could all come. I'd love to think that you've all made a new friend while you're here.' Of course this is not essential, but for me it sets the seal on my hospitality. And it does create the atmosphere in which people feel they've been given the go-ahead to talk to strangers – to network. I ask everyone to make sure they sign my guest book before they leave, encouraging people I don't know well to leave their full contact details.

A party too far

Finally, a warning note. As far as parties go, I know I go too far – quite literally, sometimes. I was at a political conference in Blackpool, but determined to attend an important business reception that same week in London. I caught the early morning train out of Blackpool, went to the party and returned to the conference at crack of dawn the following morning. Predictably, I was utterly exhausted, unable to make a worthwhile contribution at either end. Being so tired I quite lost my sense of humour. I have to remember my priorities – there are limits to how far you should go in the hope of networking, or making a new friend. The day must surely come when I learn you *can* miss a party and live!

Friendly Behaviour

Smile – think of any social occasion as an opportunity, not a nightmare

Brief yourself – have something of interest to talk about to fellow guests

Circulate, circulate, circulate – don't miss the chance to meet people and network

Never hold an all-day party – two hours is long enough

Don't worry if you've overbooked – people always drop out on the day

When friends or colleagues can't accept your invitation – invite them next time

Be bold and mix your guests – business and personal, old and young

Consider welcoming your guests with a few words – it helps them to network

5

Small Talk
overcome that shyness and make contact

I once got a rather terrifying invitation from a posh newspaper editor to attend his drinks party. I knew that everyone there would be hugely well informed about things I'd never heard of. But, as always, it didn't cross my mind not to accept. I promised myself that I wouldn't go into a decline if people kept glancing over my shoulder, poised to ditch me should a more important player glide by, and that I would not escape to the loo when left with no-one to talk to. Finally, I consoled myself with the thought that I need only stay for half-an-hour.

But more important still, to help me survive this impending ordeal, I took with me my secret weapon: small talk.

But what is small talk? Well, when I was producing BBC Radio 4's *Any Questions?* programme, it was the warm-up question before the show which unleashed a rush of intimacies and revelations, and really got the audience in the mood. That's an example of small talk – something that starts the conversation flowing.

You don't have to 'brush up your Shakespeare', as they sang in *Kiss Me Kate*, but I strongly recommend that you sharpen up your small talk. Deploying small talk effectively is an important social skill which is part of networking and the art of making friends. It's like mixing the paints on a palette before you start to paint the picture.

However good your intentions, you still need some help to get you through those first awkward minutes when you arrive at a social function or are standing around waiting for the start of a business meeting.

At a party, some people feel their best hope of survival is arriving when everything is in full swing and losing themselves in the crowd, but I think it helps if you get there relatively early. This gives you time to talk to the host and the few people already gathered without having to fight for their attention, and perhaps lose it. Personally I find it's less of an ordeal than walking into a room already packed with people.

But what on earth will you do if you find yourself somewhere talking to someone who is just so superior, so pleased with themselves, that you feel quite tongue-tied, with nothing to say? Or worse still, what if you end up sitting next to someone whom you're told is very important, making you feel it's up to you to impress them or entertain them brilliantly? You can't just get up and leave the table or spend the whole time looking at your hands.

Small talk is your answer.

Small talk topics

I was holding a business lunch the other day; a guest I hadn't met before was the first to arrive; he looked rather on edge. I was worried that he might be too uneasy to contribute to what I'd planned to be a lively discussion. Offering him a drink, I said I'd been interested to read in that morning's paper that a couple of glasses of wine a day could be good for your health. He perked up a bit and replied that he'd seen that article too. We were off. It wasn't a very brilliant remark of mine but it proved enough to get us talking. By the time other people began to arrive, my first guest was ready for them (and I don't mean plastered!)

Almost anything ordinary can be a suitable subject for small talk. There are, however, a few forbidden topics – not the old ones: sex, politics and religion. These days small talk unmentionables are: trouble with the builders or domestic appliances (we've all struggled with our own broken-down washing machines and blocked drains, thank you); the merest hint about how hard it is to get good baby-sitters nowadays; or the horrors of commuting to work.

Social occasions are most definitely not an opportunity for you to off-load the minor irritations of the day or list your general aches and pains. Keep to yourself detailed accounts of your unpleasant rash or other medical symptoms – or worst of all your food allergies. People are there to relax, not to re-live your hysterectomy, or your battle with acne or the boss. And keep tales from the nursery brief, to be recounted only in passing. Other people, who don't know your family, do not want to hear detailed reports of what your offspring have been saying or what your teenage children or grandchildren are up to.

Small talk does not have to be clever but it should not be banal. A good simple opener is: 'How do you know our host?'; or you can seize on something about your companion that you can be nice about: 'What a remarkable jacket' or 'I love that handbag or tie'. Or you can just look around the room and find some striking object to comment on – an unusual painting or a particularly beautiful arrangement of flowers.

Try to keep calm; other people will pick up your vibes if you look anxious – remember there are probably half a dozen people there who are equally at a loss and want to run off home too.

I have a journalist friend who now writes as an agony aunt. Many years ago, she says, while she was still nervous about going to parties, something very obvious dawned on her: 'People may not talk to me', she realised, 'but that's no reason why I shouldn't talk to them'. That simple thought has seen her through every difficult social occasion since.

Ice breakers

The fundamental thing to keep in mind is that everyone likes to be asked to talk about themselves – even the most distinguished people. I've found you seldom go wrong with questions beginning 'How …?', Why…?', Where…?', When …?', What …?' The fact is that people will think you are showing remarkable intelligence and judgement if you ask them to talk about themselves.

Remember too that everyone loves a little flattery – and it doesn't have to be particularly subtle. I invited a shy friend of mine to the drinks reception after the *Any Questions?* broadcast. She found herself nose-to-striped-shirt with a Tory Cabinet Minister who'd been on the panel. He showed no signs of speaking to her until she said simply: 'I did think you were very good on the programme'. He beamed with obvious relief that someone had enjoyed his performance. The two of them fell into a lively conversation which my friend still talks of today. Even the most important people often feel the need to be reassured, and warm to those who reassure them.

One of my friends, who is highly intelligent but not much interested in politics, told me about her experience at a prestigious black tie dinner some while ago. She found herself seated next to a rather distinguished-looking man. His face seemed familiar, but she didn't recognise him at all. She asked him what his job involved and he told her he did a lot of travelling. They had a lovely time talking about holidays and books without her realising who he was – the then Foreign Secretary. She felt mortified when she realised her mistake, but I bet he'd had a wonderful evening, for once not under the political spotlight but enjoying my friend's small talk. I think most people, however intelligent, relish the chance to exchange small talk from time to time.

It can be a good idea when you first sit down at a table, whether in a social or a business setting, to introduce yourself to your neighbours. This gets people – including you – into a talking mode. If partners are there too I try to take note of who's with whom – some don't take kindly to your monopolising their other half, so try if possible to draw them into the conversation.

Try to keep abreast of any topical subject in the newspapers or on radio or television that day that could be a good talking point; don't start with really heavy subjects like 'The Single Currency', but more lightweight things like: 'Dieting can damage your marriage' or 'Sunlight makes people happier'. It shows you keep up with things and can help you get a discussion going either with your neighbour or around the table. That's the essence of small talk – getting things going. The heavier stuff can come later.

Holidays can be a good topic of small talk, but holiday jokes, like wine and souvenirs, don't travel well, so go carefully. What seemed riotously funny when you were soaking up the sun often sounds pathetic when re-told to a stranger, or even a friend back home. On the other hand, I admit that people do enjoy hearing about your holiday disasters – hotels where the swimming pool was closed for repairs or airfares that turn out to be twice as expensive as anybody else's. It makes them feel a whole lot better.

Books are great small talk fodder. If you know you have a social occasion to attend, glance down the top ten list of hardbacks and paperbacks in the Sunday papers. All you need to know is that the books exist. It's a bonus if you can read a review or two and have a clue what they're about. Then, even if you haven't had time to read the books yourself, you can ask other people for their opinion.

As to your opening line about yourself, try to avoid: 'I'm just a housewife' or 'I'm afraid I'm only a mother'. People don't know how to react. It's much better to tell people about your current interests – perhaps you're going to an evening class or you're studying for an Open University degree or working part-time at something interesting. Or you can talk about what you did when you were working full-time outside the home. But there's no need at all to apologise for not having a current career, if that's the case. Maybe you're a full-time carer with an elderly relative or a parent with small children. That doesn't mean you're not alert to what's going on in the world.

Developing the conversation

Once small talk has broken the ice for you, don't worry if you can't find much more to say. People often prefer to give their views than to hear yours. Go on asking them questions about themselves and be a good listener.

When you begin feeling a bit more confident you can start expressing your own opinions. Just because you're not an expert doesn't mean you can't have a view. But be cautious: don't be too dogmatic. A clergyman I know told me he'd stopped wearing his dog collar on trains because he always found people wanted to lecture him about the Church of England, rather than ask him about it. So perhaps put your opinion in the form of a question rather than lay down the law, especially if you're talking to an authority on the subject.

Don't, whatever you do, ask professionals for a free personal consultation. The last thing a doctor wants to hear about, having dealt with other people's ailments all day long, is your indigestion. In the same way a solicitor doesn't want to sort out your messy divorce, a psychiatrist your neurosis or a builder your rising damp.

It's fine to talk about their area of expertise – they'll love telling you their success stories – but not to ask for specific advice. And even if it does sound pretty dreary, always try to make people feel their job is interesting. We can't all be a top surgeon or Chancellor of the Exchequer. If confronted with an insurance agent, for example, you could start the conversation with: 'I've always wondered how you weed out the fraudulent claims'. Once again you'll find people, particularly those in what appear to be less glamorous jobs, appreciate your interest

By all means have one or two jokes up your sleeve, but do be careful not to repeat the same one over and over again. That's a real danger for me because I can only ever remember one joke.

You may think I'm emphasising the importance of small talk just because I don't have any 'big talk', but I don't think so. I thoroughly enjoy joining in debates and serious discussions, and making my contribution at business meetings; it's just that the scene has to be properly set. I suspect some people are afraid that any display of a talent for small talk suggests a lack of depth. Far from it. To me it reveals a refreshing lack of arrogance and a willingness to 'connect' with people at a human level. In fact it's those with the most worthwhile things to say who are usually the ones who bother to begin with small talk. They know its power.

Small talk is more than it seems. It's the prelude to big talk. Without it, the serious stuff that follows can often be a major let-down. If I were the Secretary of State for Education, I'd make small talk studies mandatory – up to A level. And just to practise the skill I'd designate a Small Talk Day once a year – no big talk allowed. It could oil the wheels at work and transform the nation's social life.

Friendly Behaviour

Think of sentences starting 'How …?', Why…?', Where …?', When …?', What …?'

Ask people about themselves – they'll be happy to tell you

Be complimentary where you can – people will respond

Keep a list of simple opening lines:'How do you know our host?'

Don't talk about your allergies and ailments – or trouble getting to work

Don't lay down the law – especially with an expert

Don't ask professionals for a free consultation

6

Networking
for pleasure and for business

When Richard asked me to marry him I was ecstatic. But I found myself strangely reluctant to name the day. In his speech at our wedding reception Richard said that was because I was worried that in settling on a date so far in advance I might later find I was missing out on a better invitation somewhere else. I'm ashamed to say he was probably right. But so was I. As it turned out, the dates we eventually chose for our wedding and our honeymoon meant we missed a dinner with a film mogul and a drinks party in Downing Street. Just think: all those people I might have met and made friends of, all the things that might have flowed from those social encounters – for pleasure and for business!

Since I started making friends I've always had that feeling that a contact is never to be missed, because it may lead on to something else.

At the age of twenty-one I applied for the job of copy-typist in the BBC news room in Southampton. I got it. I think it must have been because I was in the communications division of the WRNR and the BBC obviously liked the sound of a 'communicator'. More significantly, I heard about that job through the friend I'd made in the WRNR; 18 months later she landed a job in commercial television through a tip-off from me. That was my first experience of networking.

'Networking?' I hear you exclaim! 'that's a dirty word isn't it?' Well, for some people it is. It conjures up a picture of a brazen social climber forcing their way into any group that may advance their prospects – busily thrusting business cards at anyone of importance they bump into. That's not how I see it; for me networking simply means putting people together. I've never been able to draw the line between business and pleasure – I think of all my friends and colleagues as people who may enjoy meeting each other. If the encounter turns to friendship, or leads to a new job, that's just a bonus.

Not long ago Richard and I held a dinner party in which we included the girl who had first brought us together at a television conference, and our next-door neighbour, a single man. Rather to our surprise they stayed late, still absorbed in conversation with each other. Within a year we were delighted to be invited to their wedding.

So for pleasure and for business, networking your friends should become part of your daily life. Abandon any thought of jealously keeping certain friends just for yourself. Your friends obviously find you interesting and worthwhile; there's no reason to keep them from people who will perhaps offer them something in addition.

Cast your net wide

I find it fascinating to see my friends mixing together – I discover a new aspect of them as they rub up against each other. I'm sure my friends see another side of me too when I'm with their friends.

The best friendships are those where each of you brings out the best in each other. But just because someone works well with you doesn't necessarily mean they will work with all your other friends. So don't waste time worrying whether certain people will or won't get on with each other if you introduce them. That's their problem. They don't have to see each other again. And I've found that if you do unwittingly bring together people who dislike each other, they rarely make a scene.

At one of my get-togethers recently I enthusiastically introduced two women only to hear one of them acidly remark: 'The last time I saw *her* she was coming out of my husband's bedroom!' I'm pleased to say they both stayed put and there was no row, though I couldn't claim to have made them the best of friends.

On another occasion a friend brought along a well-known right-wing historian who'd recently made himself very unpopular with his views on the Holocaust. Lots of my Jewish friends, who happened to be there, were out-raged, but again no-one made a scene and several of my guests seized the opportunity to tackle him about his ideas.

These were extreme cases. I wouldn't have chosen to organise what might have become unpleasant confrontations, but many's the time I have unwittingly invited people who were not on speaking terms to a party where quarrels have been resolved and friendships repaired.

Mending your net

At one of my Christmas parties two television presenters bumped into each other in the crowd. One had originally worked as a young reporter on the other's show, then become presenter of something very similar herself. He'd felt miffed. She went on to be an even bigger star. They'd not spoken since. But at my party she tapped him on the shoulder and got a warm response. They were both glad to make up, and I was thrilled to think that my friendship with both of them had helped.

I think people are often only too pleased to have the chance to meet in these situations and perhaps resolve their differences. It's just that no-one has ever brought them together before and that neither of them has felt able to make the first move.

There have been times when things I've arranged have flopped miserably. You have to expect the odd failure when you're networking. I held a lunch for eight the other day – some business colleagues, some friends – and nothing went right. I hadn't put in that extra effort – ringing around the day before to check everyone was coming, for instance. In the event, one guest didn't show up. When I rang her she told me the lunch wasn't in her diary – a call from me the day before would have sorted that out. Someone else rang on his mobile to say he was stuck in traffic. A late start to the meal meant three guests had to leave before I could serve coffee. The conversation never quite got off the ground. I had to console myself by saying I'd 'learned a lesson'. In this case, two lessons: to ensure I make those essential check calls the day before, and never to delay a meal for latecomers for more than twenty minutes. Whatever happens to me in life, trivial or traumatic, I need to feel I've learned a lesson from it, and invariably I have.

Networking your friends doesn't always go smoothly. You just have to be flexible, and constantly on the alert to make sure everyone is engaged in conversation and feeling at ease.

I held an informal lunch at my flat more recently where my guests did arrive on time. But over drinks I realised that two people who were enjoying a most animated conversation were those I had planned to place next to each other for the meal. I hastily switched my seating plan around. It's a good idea to be alert to this if it's a sit-down occasion.

After people have had ten minutes or so to talk to the people sitting next to them, I usually introduce a topic we can all discuss together. But you don't have to do that. On this occasion I decided to ask my guests to tell the rest of us a bit about themselves and what they were doing.

Quickly I introduced everybody around the table, ending with the man leading an appeal for a women's cancer centre at one of London's major hospitals. That got us going. A little later I asked another guest to tell us how she was setting up a new information centre for refugees and asylum seekers. Again it was a subject everyone had something to say about. Then another friend, the founder of an organisation for improving the health of older women, said her piece. And so it went on round the table.

I think that all my guests enjoyed themselves. They left feeling they'd learned something and yet at the same time had had a chance to talk about their own interests and air their own views. There was a lot of exchanging of cards and telephone numbers: my friends were networking.

And as a bonus, I was delighted to hear a few weeks later that the man fund-raising for the women's cancer centre had asked my friend with an interest in women's health to be a patron of his charity. Networking had continued after that lunch.

Networking for jobs

Certainly networking includes helping your friends find work or change a job. If you have contacts in the area your friend is interested in, do your best to help. They'll need to have the talent to get the job, but perhaps you can advise them whom to go to.

I usually speak to the person wanting the job, then ring someone I feel could be helpful and say they will be hearing from my friend. I then ring back the friend and tell them to mention my name when making contact. That's all you can, or should, do.

And do remember this: it's worthwhile networking at all levels. I've found that whenever I've been given a helping hand, it's often come from someone who's quite junior. Chairmen and chief executives of companies, even if you happen to have met them, are usually way too high up to be in a position to make a low-level appointment or offer help, but those lower down the ladder often have the power to suggest people to their superiors. I've had offers of work come my way from youngsters I included in an event two or three years ago and who are now climbing their own career ladder.

For one of Richard's birthdays I compiled a surprise video. A colleague gave us the use of his editing suite and allocated a young trainee tape editor to put the programme together. That trainee put a lot of unpaid effort into the video and by way of thanks I invited him to my Christmas party. We kept in touch. He is now a television producer himself, and he rang the other day to say he'd put my name forward for a new television series his company was developing.

The director of one of the world's top news agencies, based in New York, told a journalist colleague of mine he'd always made a point when he worked as a foreign correspondent of getting on with the most junior assistants and officials. Over time a surprising number of them had actually ended up running their countries – they'd become a network of international contacts his competitors would have killed for.

Some people may see this as cynical, the appearance rather than the reality of friendship. I don't think so. To me, it's all about human contact, establishing friendly personal relationships with people, relationships which can be rewarding in themselves and may sometimes bring other returns that you could never have predicted.

Networking can also extend from your friends and colleagues to their offspring, but there's a proper way to do it. I was at a talk on the television industry where I knew the speaker, the founder of a new television channel for young people. My stepson was with me and wanted to offer the channel a programme idea. He asked me the best way to go about it. I suggested he introduce himself to the speaker, mentioning my name and saying he had an idea he wanted to pitch. He should then hand over his business card, and ask if he could call him the next day, trying to get his direct line and the name of his secretary. Then he would be in a position to initiate the contact, rather than waiting for a call.

This approach is best, I think: it means that while you seize your networking opportunity, you don't force yourself and your idea on your new contact at what is probably an inappropriate moment. The last I heard, my stepson had shown his pilot programme to the channel and was negotiating a deal for a mini series. Now it's down to him.

If, in the same spirit, one of your friends suggests you make contact with someone who they think could be helpful to *you*, do make sure you bother to follow up the introduction offered. You owe it to your friend to do so and it could prove useful. And whatever comes of it, remember to let the person who helped you know what happened.

The only time I'm reluctant to network is when I'm asked to recommend someone I've never met. Try to avoid doing this. The fact is that if you don't really know a person, or know how good or qualified they really are, then your recommendation is worth nothing. And if they turn out to be useless, the person you have recommended them to will certainly not think of you as a good friend any more.

That's the rule I try to stick to. However, I have sometimes compromised in order to help a friend. Once, I had a call from someone who's often helped me out when I've referred people to him in the past. He told me he'd given my name to a woman who'd just arrived back from the USA and was eager to work in television news. When she rang I tried to find out as much as possible about her past experience in television and asked her to fax me her CV. I said I'd do my best. I spoke to a colleague who said he'd be interested to hear from her, faxed her CV to another and left a voice message for a third. I made it clear to them all that this was someone I'd only heard about through a friend and couldn't recommend personally. I then rang the woman concerned, giving her the three contact numbers and explaining what I'd done. It was a chunk out of my day, but I did it as a favour to an old friend.

The more you network your friends, the more you increase your social mobility – your ability to move in lots of different circles.

Recently I was interviewed by a television producer making a series on the changing role of class in our society. He didn't quite say it, but I think he wanted to know what a girl from a corner shop like me was doing meeting, mixing and making friends with influential, upper-middle-class people. Trying to find the answer reinforced my conviction that today, to a considerable degree, who we are is a matter of whom we mix with. That's more important than whether we were born in a castle or a cottage. Unlike family, friends cut across more than one social class.

To me it's not just a matter of going up in the world. Networking gives me the chance to meet and make friends with people from all social classes and backgrounds, and I love it. I realise that, through friends, I've had the opportunity to move outside my own world: I've loved experiencing their different lifestyles and expectations.

I have smart friends who know without thinking which knife and fork to pick up first and enjoy the snootiest of surroundings, and others who lead a much less sophisticated existence on very little money; people whose lives seem to be one brilliant success after another, and others whose careers have never got off the ground at all. That really doesn't matter. What counts is that we've got something to offer each other as friends.

How I learned to network

It was my years with the BBC that first made me aware of the value of networking – of putting people together. When I moved from being a secretary to producing radio programmes such as *Down Your Way* and *Woman's Hour*

I had to get into the habit of meeting people, making contact, and establishing some personal rapport with them.

For *Down Your Way* I would arrive in a village or community and start looking for the most fascinating, interesting people there to include in the broadcast. The presenter of the programme and the recording engineer would join me a day or two later. Meanwhile I was on my own, and I felt very lonely. But I found if I put a smile on my face and made myself listen to what the landlord of the village pub or the headmaster of the local school had to say I would soon be on friendly terms with them, and they would introduce me to other people who had something interesting to say for the programme.

Little by little this approach became second nature to me; I had developed a professional skill that I could also use to make more personal friends.

During my last ten years at the BBC, I was the producer of Radio 4's *Any Questions?* series. I was in my element: now I was coming across nationally known figures I'd never dreamed of meeting before and making friends of many of them. I was learning that however distinguished or famous, my guests had the same basic human concerns as the rest of us.

At first I was hesitant about putting them together for the programme. It was the tradition each week for the *Any Questions?* panel members – four people in public life chosen for for their very strong views – to meet for dinner before the live broadcast. As the host, I was nervous about having, say, a fiery left-wing politician sitting next to the outspoken columnist of a right-wing newspaper.

Within weeks of my becoming the producer of the series, a young schoolboy gave a rousing speech at that year's Tory Party Conference. Shortly afterwards I invited him on to the programme. But I was worried. How would this sixteen-year-old prodigy manage to mix with grown-up politicians? The fact is that he was very assured and fought his corner well. Both at dinner and on air, his youthful enthusiasm added an ingredient that helped galvanise the whole team. In my programme notes I see that he didn't get E for Excellent, but did get G for Good, and was invited again. As far as the programme was concerned, the mix was magic.

I remember being particularly uptight on one occasion, when a veteran Labour MP was about to sit down with a young woman who'd just been appointed a Tory junior minister. I needn't have worried. Over dinner he politely put her at ease and even gave her a few genuinely helpful tips on how to advance her political career. It was only on air that they began to score party points against each other.

Incidentally, the best advice I ever heard at an *Any Questions?* dinner came from a programme stalwart who always told less experienced panellists: 'It's best to go on the platform with a full bladder; I find that gives your performance an added edge that gets you through the show on top form'.

Those years gave me the confidence to be bold when mixing people for any sort of gathering – for work or for fun.

Setting up a network

During my stint on *Any Questions?*, I was constantly surprised by the number of politicians who had never actually met – MP's with rooms only down the corridor from each other had often never spoken. It was the same with business people – they only met those within their own small circle. It's strange but true that many people who work in the same company, possibly in the same department even, never meet at all.

If you think that's the case in your company, why not try to do something about it? If there's a staff canteen, make a point of talking to people you meet there from other departments – you can always moan about the slow service or the taste of the coffee. Once you've made contact with someone, introduce them to one or two of your colleagues.

I was invited to speak about networking at a women's group that had been set up by someone who works in public affairs for a big company. She'd formed the group by suggesting to two or three friends in the communications field that they meet regularly once a month. She'd booked a room above a pub for their first meeting. News soon spread by word of mouth and the group has grown. She says they often call it the 'network thingy' because they don't want to be pompous about it. But networking it is nonetheless. And I see from the emails I get from the group that the women are now regularly swapping information electronically about working conditions and jobs on offer.

If you do take the trouble to start up this sort of thing, do it well. It could be good for your career – and there's absolutely nothing wrong in that – as well as increase your organisational skills. You might also meet someone who could possibly become a future business partner or employer – or a friend.

Of course networking doesn't replace talent, but there's little doubt in my mind that the person who networks has a far greater chance of that talent being recognised.

You can do exactly the same sort of networking purely for pleasure, with like-minded friends. Whether you're a young mother or whether your children have flown the nest, you only need two or three people to get the thing going. Why not, for example, start an informal club where you meet regularly to discuss, say, a book you've all been reading, or a television series you've all become hooked on?

Whatever the shared interest, you need a venue. This could be the same every time, or you could alternate round friends' homes. Then you must fix two or three dates in advance, so that if anyone misses one meeting they know when the next will be. And having dates fixed like this also means that if you meet someone you'd like to see again, you have something to invite them to.

You can start this networking on a very small scale. If, like me, you're self-employed or freelance, or if you know there are set times in your day at home (when the children are at school perhaps) that you can be free for a little while, then set aside two or three dates in your diary. You only need an hour-and-a-half at most. It could be for drinks after work, a salad lunch, a morning coffee out somewhere where they serve good cappuccino, afternoon tea and biscuits – or perhaps a mixture of all these. Then, armed with these dates, hit the phone. It doesn't matter which time or date your friends can make, book them there and then and confirm it with a follow-up note. Make sure you enjoy yourself organising it. It's all a matter of mind set – deciding you will make the most of the coming occasion.

When you've booked at least two people for each date, just forget it until you come across someone else you'd like to invite. Mix personal friends with business ones and ask if there is anyone they'd like to bring or someone they would particularly like to meet. You can also, of course, mix family and friends. If you get a good group together, now that you have an interesting occasion, think of inviting someone you've been especially wanting to get to know. No-one, however grand, resents an invitation, and even if they can't join you, you've reminded people that you're out there – networking. Many of them may be inclined to include you in something later in the year.

I'm slowly improving Richard's attitude to networking. Like most men, Richard rarely rings a friend just for the sake of it; in his case it's usually to invite them for a specific dinner or to talk about a television programme he's involved in. But lately he has got round to ringing a couple of male friends just for a chat, and then going on to invite them for a casual bowl of pasta at home. He told me he'd even thought of having them to the same lunch, thinking they might enjoy meeting each other. That's the next step!

If you've got two friends you think would get on well together, ring them and get a date they can both make, then invite a couple of other friends. Widening the occasion to include a few extra people takes off the the pressure of two particular friends *having* to like each other. As ever, it needn't be anything at all elaborate, just coffee or a drink. The introduction and conversation are what it's all about.

It's the same with a movie – you and a friend fancy seeing the same film: offer to organise it. Scribble a note to yourself as a reminder right away. Then check when the movie's showing and fix the date. As you are organising the outing, you could if you wish invite another friend or colleague from work to join you – you're now having a fun evening *and* networking!

Networking can range from recommending baby sitters to drawing a friend's attention to a job you've seen advertised; from suggesting partners for the occasional game of tennis to introducing two people who might do business together. It's all a matter of exchanging information and making connections.

That's really the secret of networking – personal contact. That's what counts when it comes to making the most of your friends – the time and effort you put into staying in touch with them directly. And, as I say, it's not just a matter of keeping in touch with your own friends. For me, the greatest happiness is when I introduce one of my friends to another and see them get on well – that brings me tremendous satisfaction.

Bearing that in mind, never promise to introduce someone and then forget to do so. Many times people say to me: 'You really should meet my friend so and so – I'll fix it'. But nothing happens. If you do make a suggestion like this, then jot down that promise immediately and do everything in your power to make sure the meeting takes place, or report back if for some reason it's not possible.

I have a friend who runs her own company dealing in the design and distribution of computer networking equipment. She's involved with an organisation of women entrepreneurs and is very ambitious, but I've noticed she's never possessive with her contacts and friends. She says: 'You can't promote yourself, so promote other women you have respect for and hope they'll do the same for you.' It's all about giving back the help that you've been given.

So do avoid being too possessive with your friends; by all means let them meet each other. Accept that your friends have their own friends, quite separate from you. And just because you like your friends, don't feel you also have to like your friends' friends. You don't.

Network on the net

Networking is much easier for us all these days now that the technology is so advanced. We can ring our friends from almost anywhere on our mobile phones – or for a far more discreet and cheaper form of communication, we can use a mobile to send a text message.

I love receiving emails: it's so satisfying clicking the 'reply' button and sending your response instantly. I'm now much more regularly in touch than ever before with my friends in the rest of Europe and the U.S.

Cyberspace chat rooms can open up a whole new world, especially for those who are housebound or unable to get out as much as they would like. And if you don't have your own computer, or are away from home, then you can drop into an internet café – they're popping up all over the world.

This is all good news. However, although this explosion of new media helps us to keep in touch with existing friends and maybe make new ones, I think it's still the personal contact that matters most. It's seeing your friend's expression, giving your friend a hug, just physically being together that sparks off ideas and conversations that you just can't conjure up online. I was interested to hear from one of my business friends that his company is relying less on electronic world-wide link-ups and going back to face-to-face meetings, even though that involves so much more travel and expense. Personal contact is what produces the best results.

With thousands of names on my database I know I'm over the top, and I admit I am sometimes overwhelmed by my inability to stay in touch with everyone on it as often as I would like. But I do love networking. And when I hear later that friends of mine have become friends of each other, it makes the effort seem even more worthwhile.

Richard does most of the cooking in our house, but I do like making treacle pudding. It's just like networking – folding in and blending your friends in to make a most satisfying mix.

Friendly Behaviour

Be generous with your friends – let them
network with each other

Don't let worries that your friends won't get
on stop you networking

Network at all levels – not just with
the bosses

Start a networking group at home
or at work

Network widely – mix friends and business
colleagues together

Leave it that you will call – take
responsibility for the follow-up

Network tactfully – make contact, then
follow through later

7

Debriefing
if you're really serious

I was arranging a lunch for one of my business clients and I needed to get hold of a particular journalist. I felt sure I'd met him at a Party political conference recently but couldn't remember his name or the name of his newspaper. I logged onto my electronic database and punched in 'Party conference' in the scratch pad. Up came about a dozen or so people I've met at Party conferences this year. There he was: I recognised his name. In my database proper, I looked him up, found his number and put a call through to him immediately. My debriefing, my homework, had paid off once again.

There is no point in building up a successful network if you can't quickly find the information that allows you to use it. You need to make sure you note and store systematically all the information you collect while you're busy networking. I call this debriefing. Debriefing is rather like brushing your teeth at night or hanging up your clothes at the end of the day – worthwhile in the long run, but easy to put off, or not do at all.

Over the years I've turned what some would think a chore into a pleasure. I've trained myself to think of debriefing as the natural and satisfying conclusion to whatever event I've attended – reception, coffee morning, conference, dinner, lunch or maybe just a chance encounter in the street or at a party. As soon as I'm on my own and have a minute or two to myself, I scribble down the names of those I've met and perhaps want to see again, together with any action points – the need to send information, make a follow-up phone call, put two people in touch with each other.

I want to be known as someone who delivers whatever I've promised. That builds a reputation worth having, and it's one I want. There are lots of people who say they'll do something, but never actually do it. I take a real pleasure and pride in delivering the goods – and in telling people I've done so!

We all know the 'Mr and Mrs Mustcomes' as a friend of mine calls them: 'Oh, you must come for dinner, lunch, drinks' – but somehow it never happens. Making a note of what went on in the thick of the action is for me the only way to do it – particularly now my circle of friends has grown. And I think this is as important for personal friendships as it is for business contacts. I debrief myself after a friend's birthday party and after a conference in exactly the same way.

How debriefing works

So – remembering the contacts you've made is vital, and following-up on promises absolutely essential.

Last week, at a mutual friend's house, a newspaper feature writer admired my embroidered cardigan and asked where I got it. It had been a present, but I mentioned a designer sale coming up the following week where I thought she'd find something similar and said I'd give her details. I made a note and sent the information the following day. She was surprised I had remembered. And I never would have done so if I'd not written it down.

I try to wear jackets with pockets big enough to hold a pen and paper. Alternatively I take a small handbag that I can sling over my shoulder that has a pen and pad that I can easily get at. (I loved it when those pens we wore around the neck were in fashion.) I jot down things such as which company someone works for or when a baby is due. I will occasionally make these notes while I'm still with someone – I think that's acceptable if you are jotting down a promise to do something, but *not* if you're merely noting down the names of the people you're talking to rather than concentrating on their conversation.

Normally I wait until I'm on my own before I pull out that pen and paper. I try hard these days not to be seen wildly scribbling notes to myself while roaming from group to group. But I'm amazed anyone can remember enough to debrief themselves properly unless they do make notes really close to the event.

Someone who obviously can is the media company chief executive who came to my flat for lunch the other day. She didn't even have her handbag with her, let alone pen and paper. I couldn't do that; I have to write things down. I'm concerned that otherwise I will forget them – and I think most of us are like that.

The fact is that most people are flattered if you make a note of something you've promised to do. I sometimes mutter reminders to myself in the middle of an event, making up little words from all the things I want to remember: **F**ind a newspaper cutting; **I**nvoice a company and **T**elephone a particular friend: I remember **F-I-T** until I have a minute to jot it all down. I'm sure I sometimes look a bit pre-occupied.

As soon as I get a moment I write out what it is I'm trying to remember: note after note of people's names and things I've promised to do. I often start scribbling as soon as I climb into my car before driving home.

Now here comes the crucial bit: once back at base I sit down with a coffee and, with the help of my scribbled notes, go through every significant conversation I've had that day and need to remember.

It really is far easier to do this debriefing sooner rather than later. I have a computer at home as well as in the office so I can update my information system at either end. A database can be kept on a simple card index or stored electronically. Whichever you choose, do make a back-up copy of some kind every so often.

If you're exhausted after the excitement of being out

and about, and just can't face feeding the information you've gleaned into your system before you go to bed, at least decipher your rough notes and transfer them clearly to a sheet of paper to be tackled first thing in the morning. I've sometimes spent hours poring over a cryptic note which I didn't transfer straightaway and subsequently couldn't make sense of.

All this is wonderful advice if you can keep a clear head. One evening recently, away at a conference, I drank far more wine than I usually do. I arrived back in my hotel room feeling distinctly fuzzy. I started to debrief but after a few minutes my notes slid from my hands and I fell asleep. The next morning I couldn't read half my scribbles – I couldn't finish my homework – I'd lost a couple of what might have been valuable contacts.

You can also enlist help for your debriefing sessions. I find it's tremendously useful at a seminar, conference or any organised event to have a list of guests in advance. It's far easier then to circulate with your guest list marked with the people you would particularly like to meet – rather like wandering around an auction or sale room with a catalogue where you've ringed what you think might prove interesting. And if you've been invited to meet any of these people while you're there then do make sure the organiser sends you their CV's in advance. If you know you're going to be talking to someone who's important to you then it's only common courtesy – and common sense – to know a little bit about them and what they're proud of.

Even if the organisers can't help you with a list of guests

before or at the event, they may well be prepared to send you one afterwards. I have often made contact with people I've only later realised were at the same event as me by saying, 'I see you were at the conference yesterday. I'm sorry we didn't manage to have a chat there; could we either meet or talk on the phone?' Missing an opportunity to network can put me into a decline for days, and this is one way I can restore my confidence in myself and make that new contact after all.

My debriefing process keeps me up to date with my friends and contacts and reminds me of what I have promised to do. And I take it a step further: I make a note of whatever other people have promised to do for me. If I've heard nothing in a reasonable time, I ring to check on progress – as I told them I would. I try to leave it so that if, by the end of the week, I haven't heard from them, they know I'll be ringing.

Making and maintaining a database

You may feel you don't have enough friends yet to justify a full blown database system, but it's still important to keep track of the friends you have in some methodical way. Apart from telephone numbers, it's essential to note full postcodes, fax, email and mobile phone details too. Only if you know how to get hold of the people you've met will your business contacts ever spark into life, or new friendships flourish.

I have an electronic scratch pad by each name in my database. I use it to make notes like: 'expert on education' or 'Tuesdays best day for lunch'. Automatically, whenever I receive any kind of written communication from anyone, I double-check my records to see that I've got their details right. I also use my database as a cross-reference. If I met Wendy at Sally's I make a note to say so by Wendy's name, and by Sally's too. In addition, I note the names of friends' partners and children.

This may all sound tedious, but it can be so very useful when you're bringing people together. By reminding you of things that are important to them, it confirms the connection and adds to the friendship you've made. You don't have to start again every time you meet.

But do avoid entering anything on your database that could be embarrassing if read by someone else, like 'can be a bore' or 'groper'. I do have a security password to stop other people using my database, but there are times when someone is looking over my shoulder at the screen while I'm working and, quite reasonably, asks to see their own entry.

With a computer you can sort your friends into different groups of people, who, say, are interested in yoga, have children the same age as yours or are experts on the tax system – then you can invite all those concerned to something together.

As for remembering your promises, before the days of the computer I kept a book on my table with a list of outstanding things to do, and crossed them out as I did them.

Now, with a computer, I have a 'priority' and a 'pending' list which work in just the same way. I delete things as soon as I've dealt with them.

So if you find out that one of your friends has moved house, put in their new address as soon as you have it – and at the same time think of sending them a card of welcome. Or if a friend has just lost their job, delete their work details and then perhaps be a true friend by ringing to find out how they're feeling and whether you can treat them to a meal.

When you're trying to phone a contact and can't get through, you should sometimes do more than leave a message. So often, I've found, messages just don't get passed on: so, if it's important, do follow up with something in writing.

Check spellings, honours and job titles before you put names in your database. If it's a business contact you might do that with the P.A. or secretary. And make sure you have *their* details too. They are the gatekeepers to the people you want to contact. If you forge a good relationship with them, they can make it so much easier for you to stay in touch with the important and busy people that you've met.

Homework like this is so worthwhile. I find it exhilarating to turn on my computer, go to the database and find everything factual I need to remember about my friends and business contacts – all accurate and up-to-date. I know how valuable that is from the number of people who ring me to ask if I can help with an address or telephone number that they haven't bothered to make a note of themselves!

For personal friends, it's a great help to keeping in touch. From a professional, business point of view a system like this is essential.

And I don't think it's a matter of turning real human beings into dry computer records. It's simply the best possible way of keeping track of your contacts and friends – and making the most of them: helping you remember exactly where they're living, what their present job is, who their current partners are, where you last met, and perhaps when you might meet again.

Friendly Behaviour

Debriefing includes everyone – friends as
well as business contacts

Keep a pen and paper handy – don't trust
your memory

Debrief while you can still read
your scribbles

Be accurate – check spellings, titles, and job
descriptions

Make a friend of the PA or secretary – the
gatekeeper

Deliver – never make a promise you don't
follow through

Back-up your contacts list – address book or
electronic database

8

The Salon
nothing grand, just getting together regularly

By the time I'd been working in London for a year or two, I was finding that my networking tactics were gradually paying off. I was collecting a lot of friends, and loved it; but I soon began to realise that there weren't enough hours in the day for me to meet up with everyone I wanted to see, as often as I wanted to see them.

I remember being on the phone one day talking to someone who was suggesting we meet for lunch. I was completely desperate, unable to see how I could fit another lunch into my diary and get through the work I was being paid for. I was beginning to fret, because I just couldn't keep in touch with all my friends.

I've always taken the view that you can never have enough friends, but now I'd gone too far.

A journalist I know came up with a solution. She suggested I start a 'salon'. Her shrewd advice was that here was a way to keep me in touch with my friends without cutting too deeply into my working day. The salon was to be my salvation. It sounds impossibly grand, and can be, but for me it's really no more than a regular get-together with friends at a set time, on a set day, in a set place. As soon as I started it, the feeling of relief was immediate. Suddenly all those people I'd promised to be in touch with, all those friends I'd rashly said I'd invite for a drink some time, all those people who rang to suggest we meet for a coffee and a quick word about a business project, could be accommodated.

I began modestly by contacting about a dozen people I'd been meaning to ring, saying 'I'm going to be in my flat for the next six Mondays between 6pm & 7.30pm – haven't seen you for a while, do drop in if you can.' I also rang one or two good friends I see fairly often and suggested they too come along to keep me company on any of the six Mondays I'd chosen. I bought a case of white wine, some sparkling mineral water (I've never moved across to still), and made a note of the six dates in my diary – just in case I forgot about them myself!

At that very first salon only six friends turned up – and three of them already knew each other. The first arrived promptly at 6pm, and I opened my first bottle. At the last minute I'd rushed out to buy crisps and peanuts, but I've got my nerve back now and stopped all that as a step too far. We stood in my front room (surely I should now be calling it a drawing room?) sipping our chilled white wine – I didn't encourage people to sit. A couple arrived together about twenty minutes later and all were with me well before 7pm.

When I first launched the salon I wasn't sure if anyone would come, but I consoled myself with the thought that at least I had phoned or dropped a note to all those people I'd long been meaning to contact but hadn't – including those friends and colleagues who'd entertained me without getting any of my hospitality in return. And then there were those I know and like but whom my husband Richard doesn't necessarily know well enough for me to invite home to lunch or dinner. For all these people the salon was the perfect answer.

The salon is different from a party. There are no formal invitations to a salon, though every now and then I'll drop to note to someone I would particularly like to come. Mostly people hear about it simply by word of mouth, or you drop it into the conversation when you meet someone you'd like to be there. It's then up to people to give you a ring to ask if they can come to your next salon or one at a future date.

At the second of my salons, two of the people who'd been there the week before returned, and one of them brought a friend they wanted me to meet. That night I entertained ten. From then on I'd find myself mentioning the salon to people I came across through my business or talked to on the phone, and by the end of the six weeks I had a couple of dozen guests walking through my door once a week, and several requests to keep it going.

My salon had become a fixture.

Now on a Monday evening at about 6pm I'm rushing to answer the front-door buzzer. I peer into the little video security screen trying to recognise my first guest and straining to hear the name shouted into the intercom above the noise of the traffic. I'm usually caught desperately wrestling with that first bottle of wine, although I try hard to open plenty of them beforehand. I've now invested in a very superior corkscrew that, if I can remember how it works, pulls out the cork with a flick of the wrist. Although I didn't choose my first floor London flat with the salon in mind, it's proved ideal. It has a lovely double aspect room – large windows overlooking two busy streets in the heart of London's Covent Garden. It's a long way from the little flat in Bristol where I first started entertaining over twenty years ago, but the philosophy of welcoming and mixing people remains the same.

There are 'regulars' who come every two or three weeks, and people I see only occasionally when they're in town; and there's usually a scattering of newcomers to the group. People come to listen, air their views on the issues of the day, gossip, exchange business ideas – and make new friends.

The wonderful thing is that anyone can run a salon. It can be as ambitious or modest as you wish, and you certainly don't have to call it a 'salon' if you find that a bit pretentious. The only important thing is to offer your friends an opportunity to drop in and see you for a moment on a regular basis.

It really is a perfect way of keeping in touch with existing friends and seeing again people whom you've met perhaps just once before. When someone says: 'You must meet so and so', instead of mentally mouthing 'But when?' you can instead instantly suggest they come to your next salon.

Salons – a great tradition

Salons have a most distinguished history, and I love the idea of carrying on a tradition where women have usually called the shots. According to Nancy Mitford the salon was invented by the Marquise de Rambouillet at the beginning of the seventeenth century. She filled her house with people chosen because they could talk entertainingly. She was not herself well educated, but had a talent for conversation and made her house so gay and amusing that everybody longed to be invited there. I'd happily settle for that. I didn't go to university and I am not well read. Richard thinks he's tackling that by reading the classics to me in bed at night. But I am addicted to meeting people – and I thrive on introducing friends to each other. All it takes is the decision to settle on a set time, a set day and a set place. Your salon can be weekly, fortnightly, monthly – whatever suits you.

It's said that when the famous eighteenth century Paris hostess Madame Geoffrin was asked 'What became of that man I used to see sitting at the end of your table?' she replied: 'He was my husband. He is dead'. At a salon, a partner, if he exists, must know his place, and my husband Richard knows his. He arrives as close to 6pm as he can, immediately grabs a bottle of wine in one hand and a bottle of mineral water in the other – he claims that stops him drinking too much himself – and circles the room re-filling glasses and lingering here and there to exchange a provocative word or two to stimulate the conversation. I have no paid help, but friends step in if they see anyone in need of a drink while I'm frantically answering the door to another guest. I feel strongly that if someone's bothered to respond to your invitation, the least you can do is greet them in person, and then make sure your new guests are introduced to a group already in conversation.

Putting people together

It's all great fun, and sometimes quite productive. My salon has nurtured a love affair between a rising star of New Labour and a young woman from industry – yes, I was invited to the wedding. My former neighbour, a budding stand-up comic, met one or two potentially useful television producers. And a successful young computer whiz kid who came with a mutual friend met one of my oldest business friends, and invited him to be a non-executive director of a new dotcom venture.

Each salon has a very different atmosphere with different conversations going on in every corner. I've welcomed politicians, authors, broadcasters and business people, together with many of my other friends and family. Each week there's usually somebody who's pleased to meet someone they'd lost touch with. And my salon seems to have become a good meeting point for friends who live at opposite ends of the country.

It was said of one of my salon hostess predecessors: 'She began by holding a salon and ended by running a saloon!' That's always a danger. I try not to say no to anyone who calls, and at times I've squeezed so many people into my flat that there hasn't been much scope for the elegance I hanker after. I'm afraid that some of the great hostesses of the past might look down their noses at my salon.

To be a successful host, the secret is to move about all the while, making sure that everyone is introduced to everyone else. You must constantly ensure that your guests are engaged in conversation, leading one away here, introducing another there. Make sure no-one is on their own and that everyone's glass is full. If someone looks extremely shy, ask them to help with opening bottles or re-filling glasses.

It's all quite demanding, but I love it.

Salon themes

I once attended a salon held on a Sunday afternoon – the hosts let it be known that over a specific number of weeks they would be expecting guests. Their salon had a literary theme: an author who had just published something would be on hand to read extracts from the book, and sign any copies bought. People wandered nonchalantly and elegantly from room to room, and most were authors themselves. But if you want to do something similar you don't have to have an author present. Your literary salon could be centred on a particular book which you encourage everyone to read beforehand – it would be a sort of mini book club.

My own salon has no particular theme, it's just a chance for different people to meet.

I try to make sure the regulars circulate and introduce themselves to newcomers. I take away all the chairs and only the elderly or infirm are allowed to sit on the sofas. Once people sit down they get stuck with each other and it's harder to move them on to meet new people.

From time to time I've been lucky enough to have a pianist or a singer among my guests, and if it seems appropriate I choose the moment to call for silence and ask my artists to perform. I only encourage this when it's something that will last for a maximum of five minutes, usually at the end of the salon – it's a good way to draw it to a close.

I was delighted to receive an invitation a few months ago from one of these performers. By day he's a lawyer, but he also writes lyrics and performs them. At my salon he met an exotic Hungarian singer who also writes music. The invitation was to a run-through of the show they've written together. It was spell-binding. I was so pleased to think these two talented people had got together in this creative way as a result of my salon.

I usually stop pouring drinks at 7.45pm, and on the whole hope to shut the door on my last guest around 8pm.

If necessary I'm not at all shy about ringing an old-fashioned brass school bell, which Richard's children bought me, and calling 'Time!' when I think we've all had enough for the evening. As with any party, I think no salon should last longer than two hours. I prefer an hour-and-a-half. Otherwise people who come and leave early are likely to miss those who arrive later. I want all my guests to have a good chance of meeting each other at some point during the salon.

You will have your own idea of the sort of friends you want at your salon. To the eighteenth century author Elizabeth Montagu, intellect was more important than rank: 'I never invite idiots to my house', she said. She held elaborate evening assemblies in Mayfair, which were known as 'conversation parties'. That sounds too much of a mouthful for me. Madame du Deffand, another great hostess, also liked to be surrounded by very clever people. But I think a complete mix is better and more fun.

Of course it's great to have good talkers and powerful personalities in your home, but I want my get-togethers to be comfortable to all – to the shy, the young, the unknown, as well as the famous, the witty and the intellectual. When guests enter my home I expect them to leave their professional hats and their importance in the world behind them and be there primarily as my friend. I try to create an atmosphere where they don't stand on their dignity or talk only to other important people in the room. That's really the bit about my salon that I'm proudest of. It may not be as classy and smart as salons in days gone by, but I do everything I can to make sure that people of every kind can meet and enjoy each other's company.

Setting up a salon

Apart from a warm welcome, what sort of hospitality do my guests enjoy? I serve a reasonably priced chilled dry-ish white wine, just good enough to stop everyone waking up with a hangover. I allow an average of half a bottle per person. I try to stick to no more than one, or at the most two, glasses of wine myself – I feel the need to be constantly on the alert, mixing guests and making a quick note of things I've promised to do.

There's absolutely no reason to serve alcohol of course, and you could make your salon a morning coffee event with biscuits, 10am to 11.30am say, or afternoon tea with cake, perhaps 3pm to 4.30pm. Whatever you decide to serve, do make sure it's ready, and that there's plenty of it – don't run out.

If you or most of your friends are away at work during the week, have your salon at the weekend. I find some people stay for less than half-an-hour, merely popping in *en route* for an evening out, others for the full hour-and-a-half – and more. I rely on people telephoning to say they will be coming; that way I know whom to contact should I have to cancel at short notice. And if too many people want to come, you have the chance to postpone them to a later salon. But, as ever, overbook knowing that it's quite normal for people to drop out on the day.

At my first salons I sometimes tried to sort out in advance exactly *who* was coming and *when* – in other words planning how I would put particular people together. That was an attractive idea, but it turned out to be a great mistake. People say they'll come, and indeed intend to be there, but often in the event fail to make that particular week. I used to find myself apologising to the person I'd lined up to meet them. Now I keep it simple – my guests must take pot-luck on who else will be joining me. Unlike a lunch or dinner party, the essence of a salon is that it is casual.

Nonetheless, before the salon begins it's very helpful to make a list, and keep it with you in your pocket, of the things you want to say to particular people you think will come. You may have undertaken to try to introduce a friend to someone you've invited who is in the same line of business, or perhaps you want to exchange a recipe with someone or take the opportunity to return a book. These things can so easily be forgotten in the whirl of organisation, and then you kick yourself when everyone's gone home and you're stuck with the borrowed book and no recipe.

Of course there will always be the guest you find you could well do without, someone perhaps you thought might be fun when you first met and invited them but now realise was a mistake – someone who comes to every salon, drinks all your wine, bores all your friends and never even says 'thank you for having me'. In the past, I understand, while favourites came and went quite casually, it was the convention that if a hostess wished to indicate that some-body should not visit her salon again without a further invitation, then she herself would conduct that person to the door. A modern hostess I'm sure would find that few of her guests would take such a delicate hint!

What I have, very occasionally, had to do is say simply 'I want to welcome some people who haven't yet had a chance to be here, but I'm so short of space; I wonder if you would give the next few salons a miss?' That seems to do the trick.

Incidentally, it's pointless being upset if someone brings a stranger you don't take to. You just have to suggest tactfully to that friend that they don't bring that person again.

I find my salon really exciting. I love seeing people who would otherwise never have met each other exchanging cards and phone numbers. And I'm so pleased to get the messages in the thank you notes and telephone calls that often arrive next day. I keep a book by the door, so that any-one I don't know well can leave me their contact details and maybe the odd comment.

The only essential for starting a salon is to like people – or at least to be prepared to like people for that one-and-a-half-hours the salon lasts! You must be ready to listen to others, to enjoy conversation and to be happy to introduce your friends to one another. And you must make sure your salon is welcoming to everyone equally.

Remember your guests have come to see you – anything else is a bonus. On one occasion, I remember, only two people came, and yet I still found that salon thoroughly enjoyable in its own way. A 'crushed' salon on the other hand has its own exciting atmosphere: I have squeezed around a hundred people into my flat. But ideally I like a salon of around a dozen or so people – that means I can greet everyone, and have time to circulate and chat to them all.

These days everyone is so busy, especially the women who might once have been natural salon hostesses, but that in itself is a good reason for a revival of the salon. The busier you are the more reason to do it. It's a wonderful way of getting together all those people you need to meet for perhaps just a few minutes' chat, without having to put aside time you really just don't have for masses of individual meetings. And if someone suggests you meet one of *their* friends then you can reply 'Do bring them to my salon'.

One of my American friends who came to my Covent Garden salon was very excited by the idea. Now she's been made Managing Director of a bank based back in the States she's asked me to help her start up a salon in New York. With the help of another American girlfriend of mine (she runs her own headhunting company) I'm going to give it a go. I hope the idea spreads – worldwide!

Being a salon host is tiring work – meeting and greeting and continually bringing friends into different conversations. But it can be great fun and you'll receive invitations to other parties in return – though that can rather eat into the time you thought you were saving. Don't be put off by the effort that's needed.

If, like me, you work from home you can find yourself isolated and lose confidence in your social skills. The salon is a perfect way to re-connect with people and make new friends. You could start with a run of, say, just three or four salon dates, and re-start later if you wish.

A salon hostess is seldom powerful, but can certainly be influential. You get your satisfaction from being a catalyst, seeing others meet, talk and get to know each other because of you – it can be magic, exhilarating. And all this in return for just being at the same place, at the same time, on the same day each week, fortnight or month.

It's well worth the effort.

Friendly Behaviour

Choose a set day, time and venue – make it easy for your friends to remember

Make sure *you* answer the door – welcome your guests personally

Don't let your salon last too long – otherwise your friends may miss each other

Make sure that whatever you're eating or drinking is ready and doesn't run out

Make a list of things you want to say to different guests – and keep it handy

Keep a visitors' book by the door and ask your guests to sign in with their details

9

The Snub
how to survive it

We've had the sweet: now the sour cream to go with it.

At a friend's fiftieth birthday party recently, I found myself sitting between the host and a once well-known actress. I spent the first half of the dinner talking to my host on my left, then turned to talk to her. I struggled. At every topic I introduced (she brought up none) she merely smiled, nodded her head in a haughty, vague sort of way and looked around the room as if for escape. After about ten minutes of this I took her firmly by the arm saying 'You're obviously very bored sitting next to me, do please let's swap seats; then you can talk to our host and I can chat to your neighbour.' She immediately protested, said she was sorry she was somewhat distracted that evening, and at last began behaving properly.

The horror of The Snub!

However skilled you're becoming in making and networking your friends, I won't pretend that it is always easy or trouble-free. You wouldn't believe me if I did. We all know that there are times when a friendly approach is rudely rebuffed, or so coolly received that you go away absolutely crushed, swearing that you'll never try to be friends with anyone ever again.

Don't give in, give up or go under.

On the whole I have always found that people respond well if you make a truly open and friendly approach to them. But there are always some who, for whatever reason, just at that particular moment want to put you down. So in this chapter I'm passing on some advice on how to deal with those unfriendly people who snub you, and how to make sure that they don't stop you going on being a friendly networker yourself.

The biggest trouble with The Snub is that by the time you realise it *is* a snub, the moment for you to make a suitably snappy rejoinder has often passed. You're left slowly turning red, first with embarrassment and then with rage, that you weren't quicker off the mark with a witty and crushing response.

Sometimes it's only when I get home and am soaking in the bath that The Snub hits me, or, even more infuriatingly, when I'm re-telling the story to one of my friends and they kindly spot The Snub for me.

I feel sure I'm snubbed much more often than I know – all those times when I'm speaking to someone when suddenly they cut me off abruptly to grab a word with some grand politician or head of industry. I sort of know it's happened but try to dismiss the thought as my imagination. And then there are the occasions on which I've approached someone I know with a big smile on my face only to receive just an abrupt nod of recognition before being ignored. I'm hardened to that now, but it still hurts when it happens.

Of course there are times when you're deep in conversation yourself with someone you've been desperate to catch for weeks and you really do need to finish that chat. But there are ways of signalling this that mean you need never resort to The Snub yourself.

Don't be put down

I have a friend I much admire who deals with The Snub beautifully. When someone tries to rubbish the popular women's magazine she edits she just looks the person straight in the eye and says in a very calm, cool voice – with a condescending smile: 'Do you really think so?' That's it, nothing more, and then she immediately turns to someone else for conversation or just wanders off. She invariably finds the snubber scurrying around the room after her trying to explain themselves.

Or you can tackle The Snub head on: 'That sounded a bit rude, rather a put down; was it meant to be?' After all, if you're going to be on the receiving end of The Snub, it's wise to make sure you're not mistaken, that it really was intended. I've often found that, when challenged people will retract what they've said and feel flustered themselves. I've actually rather enjoyed that.

But unless you really admire the person giving The Snub, does it even matter? After all, it shows *their* lack of manners, not yours. On the other hand, it if comes from a friend, have it out with them there and then, or call them later for an explanation.

The fact is that when you've been snubbed once or twice you won't find the experience so upsetting. Once you accept The Snub as inevitable, something we all experience from time to time, you can cope with it: at most you're only going to feel dreadful for twenty-four hours!

I remember the husband of a colleague bumping into me at a party and saying snootily: 'Did you make a conscious decision to keep that Cockney accent?' (I picked it up from my father). I said the subject had never crossed my mind, but if it had, the answer would have been 'Yes'. He looked rather taken aback, but I was glad I'd responded positively.

One snub still makes my colour rise when I think of it. I rang the office of a well-known newspaper columnist; I wanted him to take part in a seminar. I put in my request and added: 'He knows me because I invite him to my Christmas party every year'. 'Yes,' the secretary replied loftily, 'And he always asks, "Who is Carole Stone? I don't know her." ' I was so taken aback I laughed out loud, but once I'd put the phone down I was mortified. I'd been well and truly snubbed.

I bumped into the journalist concerned some months later and I told him about the call. Now it was his turn to feel embarrassed as he assured me he indeed knew who I was. He apologised and said that he had a loyal though rather fierce secretary. I could have left it at that, but I decided to ring the secretary to tell her I'd come across her boss recently and had made sure he knew who I was for the future. It was a friendly call and all was well, but the incident did make me realise that you shouldn't be put down in any way at all if The Snub comes at second hand.

I've wasted a lot of energy getting into a state about snubs that may never have happened. Sometimes people are just preoccupied rather than rude: give them – and yourself – the benefit of the doubt. I was at a conference, trying to catch a press officer's attention to ask her about a reception later that evening. She saw me but said she couldn't stop to talk as she had to meet someone elsewhere. I felt the colour rise in my face. Had I been snubbed? Half-an-hour later a colleague told me she'd just seen the woman in question who'd asked her to tell me how sorry she was that she'd had to rush away, and that she hoped we could speak later. My mood lifted. She had obviously realised that she'd been a bit sharp and was sorry. I hadn't been snubbed. I should have given her the benefit of the doubt, and not wasted thirty minutes feeling cross and unhappy.

As someone who's constantly on a diet, I'm vulnerable to The Weight Snub. As I grow older the battle of the bulge is more and more of a pain: I can't seem to win. At my age I have to choose between my bottom – not too big – and my face – not too lined. I can't, it seems, have both. It's those communal changing rooms in the High Street stores that really defeat me: 'We don't do that in a size 16,' says a haughty stick insect or 'Have you tried the skirt with an elastic waist?' It can take me days to recover my self-esteem after a snub like that!

I was in the ladies' room at a glitzy dinner, attempting to repair my make-up – I would pay a fortune to any hotel that would rip out those horrendous, glaring, harsh lights that show up every flaw. 'Hi Carole', cooed my 'until-that-moment' friend: 'You're brave to wear that dress: good on you'. It hurt because she was right: I had put the dress on in defiance of my spreading hips (I was in an eating phase) and already regretting it. 'Richard loves me in this', was all I could muster. Pathetic. I should have tugged the dress down gamely one more time and said firmly: 'I think you've got a point'.

If you do call on your partner or another friend for sympathy when snubbed, do make sure you let them know when, and if, you've forgiven the culprit. Richard and I met a girlfriend of mine a while back who I was convinced had snubbed me at a party – she'd ignored me the whole evening. I'd told Richard. He was furious. Since then I'd spoken to her on the phone and she'd persuaded me she just hadn't seen me. Richard, however, not having been told this, was still seething on my behalf and gave her a most baleful glare. I had to put him in the picture quickly.

The Snub can be especially annoying when it comes from someone you can't escape. I was at a dinner, stuck at the end of the table, with only the man on my left to talk to. He was infuriatingly evasive: he thought it clever not to answer any of my questions sensibly, making conversation terribly hard work. I knew the woman two seats up was his wife and I decided to be bold. I leant across to her: 'I can't get your husband to give me a straight answer,' I said loudly. 'Is there a tip you can pass on about how to deal with him?' She laughed, he looked sheepish, and apologised.

It can be ghastly if you find yourself at the dinner table stuck between two people, each leaning away from you talking to the person on their other side. In that situation I take a long time to pour myself some water, or hopefully something stronger, study the menu card if there is one, and try to seem occupied, looking vaguely in the direction of one of my neighbours and giving the occasional nod to suggest I am being included in their conversation. If that fails, then my advice is to incline yourself towards one side until they are forced to include you in the discussion. Alternatively, try to start up an animated conversation with anyone else at the table within earshot.

What really demoralises me is when the two people on either side of me talk across me, ignoring me in an even more obviously humiliating way. To begin with I just listen in, but if this rude snub continues for more than a few minutes I think your only recourse is to let yourself get cross enough to interrupt the flow of conversation, and suggest you change seats with one of your thoughtless neighbours.

And incidentally, if you ever spot someone else being snubbed in this sort of way at your table, that's your chance to prove yourself the very best of guests by intervening – and maybe making a new friend at the same time.

Often people who snub others are insecure and terrified of being snubbed themselves; they're just picking on you because it makes them feel better. It's no justification, but if you remember that, it can make you feel less upset when you're on the receiving end of their rudeness.

The office hierarchy often leads to snubs, and it's difficult to deal with. If the boss treats the deputy badly, the deputy is likely to do the same to the rest of the team. I wish I'd known that when I was a junior secretary in a small family business. It might have taken the edge off the snubs that came my way. One of the other secretaries just couldn't resist putting me down. I remember once the office staff were showing each other what our own bosses had given us for Christmas. This particular secretary had received some superb gift: 'Just exactly what I wanted,' she boasted. I unwrapped the box of handkerchiefs my boss had given me. 'Oh I saw those on sale in Marks & Spencers last week,' she said. 'They were marked down to half price and they weren't that expensive to start with.' She was right, and I was mortified. I can still recall that put down, that snub. But we worked closely together and I thought it better not to fall out with her. So I did nothing. But the snub still rankled. Later I learned that this particular woman was having a hard time herself at the hands of the Chairman's secretary. She was just taking out her own humiliation on me. When I understood that, I felt better.

It's difficult to have a come-back to a snub from someone you're trying to do business with. You've got somehow to stay on good terms. I invited one particular person to a business lunch, who'd already let me down at the last minute on two occasions. He did the same thing this time, without even ringing to apologise. I took a big gulp, and picked up the phone to invite him for the following month. He was brusque, said this was not a convenient time to talk and that I should call again. Then he slammed down the phone. That was certainly a snub, even giving him the benefit of the doubt. I felt like a scolded school-girl, but he was someone I knew would be a great guest at a particular lunch. I waited 24 hours until the effect of the snub had subsided and rang him back. We set yet another date. Whether or not he regretted his previous bad behaviour I don't know, but this time he did turn up and gave a great performance. His snub now seemed unimportant.

Sharing a snub with a friend who really is on your side takes much of the hurt out of it – rather like a dock leaf applied to a nettle sting. And if someone tells you about their snub, be honest about yours. That way you both feel better.

But whatever you do, don't go through life expecting to be snubbed, and when it does happen, don't let the experience deter you from trying to make new friends. Carry on networking.

The Pocket Snub Book

Here's my own personal Pocket Snub Book – I refer to it mentally in all snub emergencies:

To a sarcastic snub, commenting on what you're wearing: *'This outfit has had so many compliments today, I think it can cope with that.'*

To a lordly snub, from someone who thinks they're better informed than you: *'Do you really think so ...'* plus a condescending smile. Nothing more – just wander off.

To a petty snub, hardly worth the effort of reply: *'Well, I'm glad you've got that off your chest ...'*

To a startlingly outspoken snub: *'Listen Sunshine, what do you mean by that?'*

To a very rude snub, obviously intended to hurt: *'I'm so sorry you're feeling a bit off-colour today.'*

To a deep snub, one that takes your breath away: look them straight in the eye, and say, *'What satisfaction has that remark given you?'*

To a snub that you recognise has more than a grain of truth in it: *'I think you've got a point.'*

Friendly Behaviour

Confront the snubber and make them
look foolish

In business – put the snub behind you and
keep in contact

If the snubber is someone you don't rate,
don't worry about it

If it's a snub from a friend give them a ring
and sort it out

Don't accept a snub at second hand – check
it out first

In the office – remember the snubber could
be a victim of The Snub too

Share a snub with a friend – it takes the
sting out of it

Don't let a snub put you off trying to make
friends – keep on networking

10

Honesty
are your friends ready for the truth?

It was Christmas morning, Richard and I were still in bed and I was excitedly unpacking my stocking. I pulled out a large box of glacé fruits. Richard had bought me some on our first Christmas together and I'd cooed with delight. I hate glacé fruits, but now I was getting them every year and most birthdays. I looked across at him – and once again cooed with delight.

A tiny cameo, but I think it's very hurtful to be too honest about gifts whether they're from your partner or from your friends.

A good friend gave me a sweater in a colour which I absolutely hated. As tactfully as I could I told her so. She urged me to take it back and exchange it for another colour. I did. I was now delighted with her present, but I can't help feeling my friend was a little bit hurt that I hadn't liked what she had especially chosen for me. Perhaps I should have stuck with her choice, even if I scarcely ever wore it.

But what about telling the truth to friends on important issues? I have agonised over this question and come to the conclusion that on the whole you should err on the side of saying what you think your friend wants to hear. Often, people already know the honest answer, but can't bear to admit it to themselves – certainly not just yet. So I don't think there's any point in ramming the painful truth down their throats before they're ready for it.

This runs counter to the way I was brought up. My father, a soldier, was blunt, direct and honest. That's what I admired about him. That's the way I prefer it. But where friends are involved, you can't just please yourself alone, or you're liable to hurt somebody and ruin a friendship. You have to tread carefully.

A great friend of mine, a deputy features editor, was applying for the editor's job. I was very fond of her and admired her administrative talents, but I didn't think she was really up to the top job – and I knew her bosses didn't think so either. What to say to her?

In the end I encouraged her in her determination to apply for the job she wanted without telling her that I didn't think she either would, or even should, get it. It seemed to me that nothing would be served – certainly not our friendship – if I tried to stop her in her tracks by telling her no-one thought she was good enough. She didn't get the job, and if I'd been more honest I might have spared her that disappointment. But now I'm networking to find her something else more suitable to apply for, and we are still the best of friends. I hope I did the right thing.

The listening friend

'Man trouble' is a particularly tricky area between friends. Your close girlfriend is convinced her fellow is passionately in love with her – it's just, she says, that he finds it difficult to commit himself, and is not the sort of person who bothers to send birthday cards or Christmas presents. 'Oh really?' you long to scream: 'Could it be he's just stringing you along, preening himself on the way you are prepared to put up with his shabby treatment of you?' Put this into words and there's a good chance your friend will tell you, first, that you've no idea what he says to her in private (you can't argue with that); next, that she knows he's madly in love with her; and finally, that what she's hearing from you is not what she expects to hear from a true friend.

These are signs for you to adopt the listening role.

As 'the listening friend', you can expect to hear endless replaying of each exchange between the lovers, every sentence put under the emotional microscope and thoroughly examined: the tone of voice, each look, interpreted for signs of love. I know: I've done it myself. I must have sorely tried the patience of my friends, who let me bend their ears for hour after hour. But that unleashing of the pent-up agony inside me – that constant tight, sick feeling in my tummy – did help to dull the pain. And when I was ready, and hopefully before my friends had had their friendship tried beyond the limit, I did concede that perhaps after all whichever man I was agonising over at the time was a lost cause. It was a major breakthrough for me just to entertain the idea that there could be a life without him.

So even when you feel your friend not only needs but could now cope with a long overdue dose of reality, take it gently, with a 'perhaps, maybe, don't you think?' Raise the faint possibility that he's not necessarily besotted with her – the chances are she knows that in her heart already.

But beware the booby trap. Sometimes a friend will complain to you about her partner's unreasonable behaviour. Be warned! If you nod too vigorously in quick agreement you could come unstuck later when the partner is suddenly back in favour and the pair of them are inviting you to dinner. Or not inviting you.

Try instead to remain sympathetically neutral – a murmur here, a murmur there. It's safer for your friendship.

Be tactful with the truth

If a friend asks for an honest opinion about their appearance, I think you're on slightly safer ground. If a dress looks a mess or the tie's all wrong, say so tactfully. It's all a matter of taste of course, but if you've been asked for your view that's fine. If you haven't been asked, best keep your opinion to yourself.

Mostly friends only want you to endorse whatever they've already decided. If your friend has just had her hair cropped there's not a lot to be gained by saying how much you preferred it long. Tact is the essence; friendship is not necessarily a licence for blunt speaking.

Competition amongst friends sometimes makes it difficult to be honest – for example if you are both trying to reach the same goal at work. Even in your inner circle of friends this can happen. I applied for a public appointment advertised recently, but a friend of mine then asked me to put in a good word for her – she was after the same job. I explained the situation, saying that if they didn't want me, she'd be my choice. I then sent her some briefing notes that I'd got hold of and thought that she too would find helpful. She was surprised and pleased to receive them. In the event my friend had an interview but didn't get the job; I didn't even get an interview. But best of all we remain firm friends.

A television newscaster friend has given me his own story about honesty – and my Christmas party. He says the first time he received my invitation he immediately rang a newscaster colleague to ask if he would mind reading the news that night instead of him. He only explained why when, a couple of days later, the colleague received his own invitation from me. Today my friend admits he'd been less than honest: 'I'd been a bit of a sneak,' he says, 'and I was caught out'. Since he can't pull that one again, he flatteringly tells me that the night of my party has become one of the rare occasions when neither he nor that particular colleague will be bringing us the national television news.

Money and honesty can be a problem in friendship. For example, what do you do when one of your friends writes asking you to buy some very expensive tickets to a charity event that you are not the least interested in, and perhaps can't really afford? You could just ignore the request – not reply. But that risks giving offence and endangering a friendship. I usually deal with the problem by saying I don't want to buy tickets, but that I am sending a small donation to the charity instead.

I have to admit that I've borrowed from and lent money to friends in the past, but it should be avoided if at all possible. As Shakespeare writes, 'Neither a borrower, nor a lender be; for loan oft loses both itself and friend …' Rather than lend money, it's far better to give a small amount instead. Either friends become upset and angry when they find they can't repay the loan as promised, or you, as a lender, are irritated at seeing your friend spend money on what you consider luxuries instead of paying you back first. It all leads to embarrassment and bad feeling on both sides. You may eventually think there's no option but to be honest and demand your money back, with the risk of losing your friend. The alternative of course is to write off the loan, but not even that will guarantee you keep your friend.

But there are other ways of dealing with this awkward situation.

A friend of mine wrote to the person she'd lent money to with a suggestion: she knew he was finding it impossible to pay the money back; she would be happy, she said, to forget the debt if he would change his will so as to leave the money he owed to a charity she was particularly keen on. He was delighted to accept the offer, and the friendship has survived.

Now this is really important. Never *ever* be honest when it comes to your girlfriend and her weight – unless you think her health is in great danger. I've made the mistake of telling someone she should go on a diet, and it took me months to regain her friendship. Stay silent. We all know when we need to lose weight; we don't need anyone to remind us, even if we say we do. Nor do we want to be told, after months of dieting, that we've lost too much.

A really good friend once managed to make me feel quite crumpled: 'You're too scrawny,' she said bluntly, 'and it doesn't suit you.' Now possibly she was right, but we'd both been saying we should go on a diet. I had. She hadn't. I'd been starving myself to lose half a stone (I'm constantly fighting against a hearty appetite and greed). I felt that if she had really needed to tell me what she saw as the truth, she could have phrased it better: 'Don't get too slim, you're about right now' would have been less hurtful.

The real test of honesty in a friendship is when your friend discusses her partner's possible infidelity. She's suspicious and demented. You think she probably has cause to be.

This is a tough one. I have never actually told a girlfriend I think her partner is being unfaithful, even if I've suspected that is the case. The most I've done, if asked, is concede that it does look as if he's acting suspiciously.

Even to hint at any criticism of a partner is liable to cause an explosion. I got myself into trouble when, after some thought, I told a girlfriend that I'd heard the new man in her life had a well-established reputation for turning nasty. She wrote me a letter saying she loved her partner and for the sake of our friendship hoped I would not mention such things to her again. I think she was right and that I was wrong. On balance I should have kept my nose out of it. It would have been entirely different if she'd raised any worries about her partner's behaviour with me – then and only then, I think on reflection, would it have been right for me to have passed on what I'd been told, and been completely honest.

There's no doubt about it: being totally honest with your friends really is fraught with danger. Think twice before you utter those words: 'I'm only telling you this because I'm your friend …'

Friendly Behaviour

Don't force the truth on your friends – wait
till they're ready to hear it

Beware the booby trap – don't rubbish your
friend's partner prematurely

Never be honest about your girlfriend's
weight unless her health's in danger

Lending or borrowing money can ruin a
friendship – do your best to avoid it

11

Sitting Down To It
at lunch or dinner

I'd just left the BBC, moved to London and was trying to work from home. There wasn't much money coming in. I was worried that now I no longer came across my friends and colleagues through my work, I might lose touch with them altogether. To be blunt about it, if I wasn't any longer in a position to put them on *Any Questions?*, would they still want to see me?

I remember about this time phoning No. 10 Downing Street about a charity event. 'Carole Stone?', said the operator. 'Carole Stone from where?' 'Carole Stone from nowhere', I heard myself mumble forlornly. From then on I was known to the formidable No. 10 switchboard – or 'Switch' as it's respectfully referred to by those who call it more often than I do – as 'Carole Stone from nowhere', which is rather how I felt in those early days in London. But I didn't give up trying to bring people together.

I have a photo in my office of one of the first informal

lunches I ever held in my own flat in London. The faces that smile out at me include a very senior television executive, a world famous fashion icon, two women MPs and my pop idol from the 1960s, now a successful businessman.

That photo represents my little triumph: my TSL's – Tuna Salad Lunches.

In those days I certainly couldn't afford to take anyone to a restaurant. Lunches at my flat-cum-office seemed the only solution. There was one snag to that – I couldn't cook. But I could make a mean tuna salad. It was a dish I served up twice a week, Tuesdays and Thursdays, for five years – and it served me well.

I reckon that tuna salad took me twenty minutes to prepare – I got it down to a fine art. Supermarket shop at 9am, back to boil the eggs and French beans, leaving them to cool. Then at mid-day tear open the bags of lettuce, and chop the spring onions, tomatoes and avocado pears – someone always rang with a query just when I was in the middle of it, hands all messy. Then throw in the two tins of drained tuna and black olives, season, and at the last moment add the dressing. The only thing I used the oven for was to heat the bread rolls. I bought half a pound of cheddar and a chunk of Stilton to follow the salad.

I calculated at the time that I was feeding the country's 'opinion formers' for just £4.19 a head plus wine and water.

And they tucked in perfectly happily. To be honest I don't think they even noticed how simple the meal was. They were there to meet other interesting people and to have good conversation. And I was bringing them together. That to me is the fundamental basis of networking.

Take eight people and mix well

Looking back through my guest book, I am pleased to see that I stuck to my instinct and mixed people of very different backgrounds together. At my table of eight, I had senior politicians and some rising political stars. There were trade union leaders, journalists of every kind, business men and women, my mother and other relations, and people from around the country with no special reason to be there except that they were my friends.

Whether they came by taxi or public transport, or whether their chauffeur was blocking the little street I lived in with some enormous car, didn't matter a bit.

I found the diversity of my guests a positive bonus. The mix encouraged the experts – those at the top of their profession – to put what they had to say in language we could all understand. And people who knew all about one area of life got to know more about another: business people about politics, politicians about business, journalists about both, and my less high-powered friends about everything.

If anyone cancelled on the day, I'd ring round until I found a replacement – I could never bear an empty place at my table – someone, somewhere out there could be sitting here instead, making a new friend. The busier the person, I found, the more inclined they are to take you up on a last-minute offer if they happen to be available. I love last-minute invitations myself.

Entertaining a group of people at lunch can be inexpensive, not too time-consuming and great fun.

It doesn't have to be a week-day lunch; it could be on Sunday, or perhaps an informal mid-week dinner. The important thing is to have some dates for this in your diary, so that you can invite people you meet. It may be you keep it to just three or four people on each occasion.

Because of my years at the BBC I've ended up with some top people on my guest list, but it doesn't have to be like that. The principle remains the same at whatever level you're operating, whether it's for business or personal pleasure – or, as I like it, a mixture of both. You can mix and match people from very different worlds and you don't have to put on a banquet to do it.

The vital extra ingredient that makes this a successful recipe is you and how you put your guests at ease. So how do you get them to relax and if necessary to hang up their professional hats and enjoy the whole occasion as real human beings – as friends?

It's all down to you the host setting the mood – the atmosphere. And that applies no matter whether you're all sitting round the kitchen table for something simple or giving it the works with a dining table gleaming with your best knives and forks.

First of all, numbers. I think six or eight is an ideal number for a lunch or dinner. With six it's slightly easier to keep one conversation going that involves everyone. However,

I usually invite eight, because if even two people drop out at the last minute, you still have six round the table.

The sensible way to start your invitations is to ring the two or three people you really want to see and then, once you've sorted out a date with them, to try the next guests on your list. Of course if your aim is to bring two or three particular sets of people together it takes more organising – asking people to keep a few dates free for you while you try them out on the other guests. I find it's ideal to mix a couple of new faces with people who know each other – it adds to the excitement of the occasion.

Don't let food dominate

When it comes to planning your food, let my TSL – my tuna salad lunch – be your inspiration. Whatever food you decide to offer, however complicated it is to prepare, don't let it dominate you on the day. Never let cooking distract you from your friends.

For entertaining at home in my single days I relied on one or two trusted dishes. Now I've had the good sense to marry Richard, who likes cooking. But we still keep it simple. We usually start with something cold before the main course, followed by a simple pudding, with cheese for those who want it. And, just to make sure we don't give our friends the same food every time they come, I keep a book which reminds me who came and what we ate.

Of course the meal can be as exotic as you like. It's

wonderful to be offered really good food that the host has taken trouble over, but don't kid yourself that providing the most amazing meal will make you new friends. It won't. What matters on the day is that you as host aren't stuck in the kitchen doing complicated cooking when you should be entertaining your guests. Your place is with them, making sure the conversation is buzzing and that no-one feels lost or out of it. People are there to connect with each other, and they need your help.

Incidentally, while we're on food, it's a friendly gesture, when confirming your invitation, to check whether there is something one or more of your guests simply can't eat. It can be irritating if they tell you there is, but it's far better than somebody on the day actually refusing to touch what you've prepared for them. I have an allergy to garlic, for example; it makes me ill, and I try to remember to tell my host well in advance. And do respond to any guests on a diet – make it easy for them by not pressing second helpings or puddings on them; it's not a friendly act. Instead, see that there's some fresh fruit on the table. I know it can be annoying when people say no to a heaped plate of what you've carefully cooked, but a comfortable guest is what you're really after.

Where to seat your friends

To make the most of your friends, work out a seating arrangement before your guests arrive. I usually stick a post-it note discreetly behind the door, so that I can take a

quick look before we sit down. I hate it when you're invited to the table and the host says 'Oh just sit anywhere'. You
hesitate, hang back and end up sitting next to your partner
or someone you've already been chatting to before dinner,
while some pushy person grabs the chair next to that most
attractive guest you might have been seated next to.

Over drinks beforehand (they shouldn't last longer
than one hour at the very most, otherwise everyone drinks
far too much) keep an eye on who's talking to whom, and
if necessary re-arrange your seating plan to make sure
everyone has somebody new to talk to. Keep partners away
from each other and avoid putting two shy people together. It does take a lot of effort, but the more entertaining you
do the easier it will become.

I prefer a table that's either circular, or square – I find it
easier to keep an eye on my guests and make sure everyone
is engaged in conversation and looking comfortable.

Once at the table, check that everyone has a full glass of
whatever you're drinking, and a glass of water too. Then I
think it's a good idea to say a brief word of welcome and
make sure everyone knows the name of all the others
round the table – late arrivals may not have cottoned on to
exactly who everyone else is. You could even give a brief
line on each of your guests: 'Roy, you're next to Mary, she's
a brilliant nurse; Tom, on your left is Ruth who's just finished an Open University degree in design.' This gives
everyone something to talk about to their neighbour, even
if they really are shy. I let everyone chat away in these mini
conversations while we eat the first course.

As soon as the main dish is on the table and everyone has got the bits and pieces that go with it, I often introduce a topic that is either in the news or that I know is of interest to all the guests. It could be anything – education, the tax on petrol, or how to handle a sulky teenager. Usually that means one conversation around the table for a while, and I'm very happy with that as long as no-one is in any way left out. If I do spot someone sitting silent I either draw them into the conversation or change the subject to something on which I know they have something to contribute.

If you've got more than eight guests at your table it's a good idea to swap people around after the main course, especially if you've noticed someone not getting on with their neighbours. If you don't feel comfortable doing this, at least you can ask your partner or someone you know really well to swap seats with you.

Over coffee, perhaps away from the table, again make sure that people sit next to someone new, so that hopefully by the time they leave everyone has chatted to everyone else. I try to be serving coffee within two hours of sitting down to eat, especially if it's a mid-week supper when people don't want to be too late to bed.

If anyone brings a present, I try to unwrap it there and then. I find flowers can sometimes be a nightmare. It's best to keep a couple of vases handy, already filled with water, so that the flowers can be put on display right away. Wine too can be a bit of a problem. If it's just a bottle party then well and good, but if you've already got several bottles of the same wine ready for the meal, it's difficult to mix in other assorted ones that guests have brought. I find it easier to exclaim how delicious their wine looks and how much I'm looking forward to drinking it on a future occasion. As for other gifts, as a guest I am always absolutely miserable if I see the hostess whisk away to some back room my carefully chosen box of chocolates – carefully chosen so that I can sample them myself! Make sure you open all boxes of chocolates that people have brought and offer them round with the coffee. Keep your own chocolates for another time.

Being a good host

A relaxed host is a must. Don't worry if things go wrong. A friend of mine served up a cold pudding which regrettably turned out to be still frozen in the middle. She kept calm, and didn't turn a hair. Her guests attacked the pudding with every implement to hand, bonding together in a team effort to extract it from the dish, one of them even rummaging in the kitchen tool drawer for a chisel. 'Pity about the pud,' remarked her husband afterwards, when the guests had gone: 'Oh, they enjoyed it,' was my friend's reply. She was right. There's no such thing as a social disaster among people whom you've welcomed to your home as friends.

Just decide that you are going to enjoy yourself, however it goes. Don't be anxious: your guests will pick up any signs that you're unsettled.

And if you've had a row with your partner just before the guests arrive, you just must make it up before the door-bell goes for the first guests. Be generous, give your partner a big hug and say: 'Let's put our disagreement on hold'. I've been to several dinner parties where you could hear the hosts carrying on their row in the kitchen. It's a miserable experience that quite spoils the whole occasion for every-body else.

At all times it's down to you to keep the show on the road, looking after all your guests. No favouritism. For example, don't even think of disappearing to the kitchen with some particularly close friend for a good old chin wag – save that for another time when just the two of you are meeting. And make sure no-one hogs the conversation – gently intervene and pass the ball to another of your guests.

Make it easy for people who have to leave early because of the baby-sitter or an early morning start, but make it clear you're very happy for other guests to stay longer – this saves the whole party breaking up because someone has to go.

And do spoil your guests. Your friends will much appreciate it if you take the trouble to say something spe-cial to them at some point – perhaps to remark on their dress or general look of well-being, or simply to ask after their family or job.

If, when your guests have all gone home, you feel, together with physical exhaustion, the warm glow of satis-faction, then the atmosphere you've created has probably worked. And some of your friends are likely to have made friends of each other too.

Friendly Behaviour

Cook what you like, but on the day don't get
stuck in the kitchen

Find out if guests have anything they can't
eat – and warn your host if you have

See who's talking to whom – make sure
everyone meets everyone else

Have a seating plan clearly in mind, but be
prepared to alter it

Gifts – put the flowers on display, keep the
wine, open the chocolates

No favouritism – don't huddle with an old
friend in the kitchen

Spoil your guests a little – say something
nice to each of them

12

Letting Friends Go
sometimes you just have to

Not long ago a nice young man came to my flat to commit murder; worse than that – a massacre. Worst of all he was there at my invitation. But as I let him in my heart was pounding. This was something that went against my deepest instincts, everything I had ever learned, ever contemplated before. Yet it had to be done: my Christmas party list of potential guests had to be reduced.

After my last Christmas party, I made the decision never again to go through my entire database of over 14,000 names to choose the friends I was going to invite. Instead, I would just select from the list of those I invited last year, plus anyone I'd seen over the past twelve months and wanted to meet again.

My friendly assassin's mission was to remove from my database the people who'd made it to my short list in previous years but hadn't in the end been invited. Of course I'm not deleting anyone from my database altogether – I could never do that – but I am recognising that I can't any longer consider every one of my friends every year as a potential guest at my annual party.

In the old days, before I had a proper electronic database, I would sit down at a manual typewriter, go through my list of friends and contacts and, if I wanted to invite them to my party, type their name on to a sheet of paper. Easy peasy. I put those I definitely wanted to invite in capital letters and 'possibles' in lower case. If I was drastically 'over' when I'd finished my list I would then only need to look through the lower case list to reduce the total numbers.

The following year I'd start all over again, looking once more at every name on my database. It took weeks of concentration. After I got a computer, my eyes would water from staring at names on the screen. Night after night I agonised over every person, consoling myself that if I didn't invite them this year, I could always put them back in again when I went through the entire list again the following year. I tried not to look at the names of those I'd crossed out – if I did I would often reinstate them. Sometimes I even got to the stage of writing addresses on the envelopes, only to tear them up because I was over the top with my numbers.

The last time I did it like this the first trawl through my entire database produced a list of around 8,000 people I wanted to invite; I went through them again and again, four or five times, until I got it down to 1,500.

I found the whole thing an agonising process.

As Richard said at the time: 'That way madness lies'. And he was right.

Sorting your friends

Three years ago the assassin transformed my life. He wrote a special programme for my computer to help me sort out all my friends and contacts. It's a very superior kind of database designed just for what I want to be able to do.

To put it simply, I can arrange my friends in different ways. For example, I now have a 'Christmas party' box on my computer screen. If I want to invite someone I'll find them in my database, and, by holding down the 'control' and 'w' keys, I'll tick their name, and they'll join the party list. If I do 'control' and 'w' again, they're off the list and out in the cold. Sometimes in the small hours of the morning I've been so exhausted that I've done a double click by mistake and someone's out as soon as they're in, or vice versa. I worry I've done that to people and never noticed.

The fact is I do want to invite as many as possible, but I just can't squeeze all my friends, or people I think of as potential friends, into any hall I could possibly afford.

And anyway, as I've discovered, having too many guests means I've no hope of shaking hands with everyone without creating a huge queue outside the door – which is not where people want to find themselves when they've come to a party.

It may seem silly to you that I spend so much time deciding whom to invite. Perhaps you don't mind not being invited to someone's party, but I go into a decline if it happens to me, and in the same way I can't bear the thought that I'm depriving someone else. For me it's not just that they've missed an occasion they might enjoy; I'm convinced that this could be the one time they might meet another of my friends who could in some way have a big impact on their life.

And it's not that I think my party is more important than anybody else's; I feel the same way about parties I'm invited to – it could be vital to my future to be there.

So what am I doing now, for the first time ever? I'm saying that if I didn't invite someone to my Christmas party last year, I'm not going to be considering them next year, unless in some way we renew contact with each other before then.

It means that never again will I look through my entire database to choose people for my party. There are thousands of friends or possible friends out there that I'm in danger of never seeing again unless I happen to bump into them or they contact me. My heart does a somersault at the very thought of it! It's harsh, but it's the only way I can cope.

So now I've given myself an additional task. At the end of every day I must 'tick on' or 'tick off' for my next Christmas party people I've just met or renewed contact with. That way the list is continually updated, ready for me to make a selection when Christmas time comes round.

How friends come and go

Quite reasonably, you may say that all this has nothing to do with you, but I think the same principle applies whether you have thousands of people on your address list or just a handful. You have to decide who you can keep up with, who you just keep in contact with occasionally and who you have to let go.

The former chairman of a major supermarket chain told me that once he's made a friend and admitted that person to his circle, then that's it: with rare exceptions that person will always be a friend. His wife on the other hand, he says, is always going off her friends until suddenly she's 'on' them again. She gets fed up or cross with them, and then they're out, and then they make up. He doesn't have these ups and downs himself.

That may just be because of the different way men and women seem to deal with friends. I think most men are probably much less dramatic about their friendships than women. But I believe that on the whole a friend should remain a friend – once you get to know what it is about them that can irritate you, you can avoid those situations where it might become a problem.

Sometimes people drop their friends not because of anything they've done or not done, but simply because they've shared an unhappy experience or a confidence in a way they now regret.

Perhaps you've been close to a friend following some unexpected tragedy. With some, as I've mentioned earlier, that's enough to make you friends for life, but for others it's an episode they can't bear to be reminded of in any way – and you are that reminder. Or maybe a girlfriend has spoken frankly to you at the time of her marriage breakdown and revealed too much about the husband she's later decided to stick with. Now she wants to forget all that, and that could mean forgetting your friendship too. It's nobody's fault and it can't be helped. But don't let go of a friend over some misunderstanding between you – tackle it head on and hope to resolve it.

Sometimes you have to change your relationship with a friend, even if you don't completely let go. This can happen if there's a new partner in your life who doesn't get on with that particular friend – it's inevitable that you'll see less of your friend from now on.

Some friends we simply outgrow: most school friends for example, those who were parents at your children's dancing class, or former colleagues from your office who have now moved on so that your paths no longer cross in the same way. Many friendships are very much based on current common interests, and once that phase has passed there's not much else to keep you in touch.

Yet you still feel you ought to send a Christmas card, and if they live nearby, you find yourself in a dilemma over whether or not to invite them round for a drink. And do you accept when they call, inviting you?

I compromise. I still send the Christmas card, but I leave out the usual line: 'We really must see something of each other next year'. As to any invitations to meet, I politely refuse, saying: 'Everything's a bit hectic at the moment but thank you so much for the kind thought'. These friends with whom you feel you no longer have anything in common can make things difficult by inviting you to something many months ahead, knowing it's unlikely you'll have anything else in your diary yet for that date. The trouble is that if you accept their invitation you'll feel obliged to invite them back. So be firm. If you really don't want to keep this friendship up, say no. Normally the overtures will cease, yet by not being rude you won't feel embarrassed if you bump into each other. And in this way, although I do let some friends go, I don't feel I've cut them out of my life forever.

Virginia Ironside, the journalist who writes 'Dilemmas' for *The Independent*, was asked to give advice the other day to a woman who said that she and her husband have lots of people on their Christmas card list that they haven't seen for years. The husband was arguing they should make the effort to see them, but his wife said she had enough friends and interests and wanted to leave things as they were. Which of them was right?

I read on, assuming the woman would be encouraged to back her husband up and regain contact with all those on the Christmas card list. Not at all. Virginia's advice was as follows:

Friendship is like juggling plates in the air. There's simply a limit to the number of plates that can be regularly spun, indeed which one regularly wants to spin, and those that fall off from lack of spinning sometimes have to start twirling themselves if they want to get back into one's life. And even then, ruthless as it may sound, there may not be room for them. Because there is a limit to the number of friends we can accommodate. Friendship, and the maintaining of it, can be hard work.

I certainly agree with Virginia that looking after your friends can be hard work. And I also agree that not all friends can be equally important. Virginia goes on to say that there's a landscape of friendship in which some friends occupy the foreground while others are far away in the distance. Again, I agree. But her advice was that the wife should do nothing to round up those distant figures, and that if her husband really wanted to do something about it he shouldn't expect her help. And there I part company with her.

I would be delighted if my husband suggested this to me, and I would certainly encourage him in his desire to see these distant friends. With this year's Christmas cards why not, as one of Virginia's readers suggested, enclose an invitation to a party? It could perhaps be held in a local community hall one weekend if you really haven't got enough room at home.

In this way both husband and wife would have the chance of discovering if there were friends out there they wanted to see much more of. I feel excited at the very thought of it!

I do accept that if some friends step into the foreground others will inevitably have to take a pace back. That's how friendship works. Some friends may well disappear from view. But if you've been close friends with someone, even if you don't see them very often, that closeness remains.

I was in Brighton recently, where one of my oldest friends lives. We shared a flat there when I was working as a BBC local radio producer, but I hardly ever see her these days. Now I was attending one of the Party political conferences and we went to a fringe meeting together. As usual we just picked up where we'd left off last time and exchanged our news. I mentioned I was writing this book. Afterwards she sent me a letter about friendship. 'It is irrelevant', she wrote, 'whether close friends see each other or not. We are in each other's heart.' I agree. You can't take those shared memories away. So whether a friend moves centre stage or off into the background I think those ties of friendship remain.

I think my answer as to when and how to let friends go is this.

You can only give a certain number of friends all the care and attention they want and deserve. I accept that. But I don't accept that means you can only have two or three real friends; I think you can have as many close friends as you've time to keep happy, and that depends on what else you've got going on in your life at any particular time. And it doesn't mean you have to abandon the possibility that you could one day renew contact with many more people you still regard as friends.

The important thing is to leave the door ajar. Never put friends down, even when you can't possibly keep in regular touch with them all. You may have to let them disappear from view, but they'll still be there, and some will reappear in your life.

Friendly Behaviour

Never be rude, but say no politely and firmly
to unwanted invitations

Send a Christmas card, but don't add 'hope
to see you soon' if you don't mean it

Don't let go of friends through some
misunderstanding – sort it out

Close friends stay friends – you don't have
to see them all the time

A shared memory of sadness can
occasionally end a friendship – accept it

If you do let go of friends, leave the door
ajar to renew the friendship

13

TLC
how to keep your friends in good running order

I had just heard that the mother of a friend of mine had died. I didn't know her myself, but I was conscious she and her son had been very close. I dropped him a note of sympathy and suggested we meet when he was feeling up to it.

I used to hold back in situations like this, thinking that my gesture of sympathy might seem an intrusion, but I have found that, quite to the contrary, it is nearly always appreciated. That letter didn't take long to write, but I know from the tone of his reply that it meant a lot to my friend.

Friends appreciate a bit of TLC – Tender Loving Care.

Richard and I are members of a very informal dining club that meets for a meal out roughly once a month. We were invited to join by friends of ours, a well-known television hostess and her producer husband. He'd been in such good form, so funny and sharp, when we'd last met for a meal that it was a great shock to us all when we heard he'd died. We went to the funeral and then the next day to the house for prayers – he'd recently converted to the Jewish faith. The dining club had been due to meet again for dinner that very evening, but no-one wanted to suggest we should stick to our plan for fear his widow would be upset. I found myself very gently testing the water with her to see what she felt. As I suspected she might, she decided that an evening meal with friends was just what she needed. We all went out together, and had a lovely time. She tells me she felt her late husband was very much with us in spirit that night.

So be brave in these circumstances; risk a rebuff, and you may well find that this is just the moment when your friendship is most appreciated. And do remember, following a bereavement, it is often in those weeks and even months after the funeral that friends need each other most. Do be prepared to persevere if a friend is not very responsive at this time. Eventually they will re-emerge into the world and be glad you are still there.

My friend said something else too. She told me that kind friends asking how she was bearing up after her husband's death inevitably reminded her again of what she'd lost. What she found more helpful was when friends offered their sympathy but went on to recall experiences they'd shared when her husband had been alive. Then, rather than answer questions about how she was feeling – inevitably up and down – she could talk about happy memories.

It's certainly no good thinking you can just sit back once you've made new friends – that's it; all done. By no means. The fact is there are no shortcuts if you want to reap the real rewards of friendship.

It's like everything else we rely on in life: don't skimp on the servicing. If you do, your friendship will break down, just as the central heating boiler does when the outlook's bleak and you really need some warmth badly. Friends have to be looked after and checked up on regularly to make sure they're in good working order: taken care of. Incidentally, that care, I've found, usually comes back to you in abundance later.

The friends etiquette

There's a 'friends etiquette' that you need to observe if you're really going to care for your friends successfully.

One of my friends is particularly good at this. When she rings she always starts by asking: 'Is this a convenient moment to talk?' Just because a friend answers the phone at home or at work doesn't necessarily mean they want to chat at that very moment – they could be waiting for an important business call, have visitors, or be deep in some television programme – I know better than to call my aunt during her favourite soap.

Any approach from a friend deserves a prompt response. I remember when I was a very young secretary my first boss stressing that whatever was in his 'in' tray could be dealt with as well today as tomorrow. Irritatingly, he was right. It's plain bad manners not to return a call as soon as possible – that's something that never fails to get me down. Your response doesn't have to be lengthy if you don't have the time for it then. All that's needed is a brief acknowledgment that you've received the message and that you'll ring back later that evening or at the weekend.

It's important to people you regard as your friends that you remember how to spell their name – first name and surname. I am 'Carole' with an 'e', and I don't react nearly as well to a letter sent to 'Carol' Stone. Make sure to ask your friends whether they are Ann or Anne, Stephen or Steven, Johnson or Johnston, and check for any letters after their names – whether or not you think that OBE or MBE is justified, it's no doubt a source of much pride to them.

It's perfectly in order after you've been to a social occasion to ring your host next day to check the name of a fellow guest. Incidentally, if you then invite someone you've met there to a function of your own, do invite the host too – at least for the first time.

The 'friends etiquette' demands that you don't take advantage.

A friend of mine gave a cocktail party and was thrilled she had an acceptance from a Bishop she had long admired. But at the party one of her other guests spotted His Grace immediately and completely monopolised him. What's more, the following week she invited him to a lunch and didn't even tell my friend, let alone include her. Loss of Brownie points there. We all resent those who make a habit of scanning the room to seek out our most interesting guest with larceny, not sharing, in mind.

And should you ever land a job through one of your friends' contacts, don't forget to let your friend know and thank them straight away. The other day I introduced a friend to the chief executive of a large privately owned company. They seemed to hit it off. Later I heard from another source that my friend had been hired by the company as a consultant for a large fee. I was delighted to see successful networking. But at the same time I was miffed that my friend hadn't been in touch to tell me.

Good manners are essential in friendship, as they are in any relationship. Just because you know your friends well it doesn't mean you can treat them discourteously.

If you're a smoker, don't light up in company without first checking either with the host or those in your group that they don't object. And don't take offence if they do – there'll probably be somewhere nearby to have a cigarette if you're desperate.

It's not necessary, but I try to take a gift, however small, for the host of whatever function I'm attending. It need only be a box of chocolates, but do remember to attach a card with your full name clearly visible. Your host probably knows several Carole's and could easily not realise the gift is from you – you deserve the credit for being thoughtful!

Don't embarrass friends, if you've invited them to some social occasion, by not giving them a hint as to what to wear. And whatever dress code you decide on, do make sure you stick to it yourself on the day. There's nothing more shaming for a guest than the host who's decreed casual wear opening the door in some glittering formal creation.

The words I dread to hear are 'smart casual'. They seem to mean completely different things to different people.

I went to a regatta one summer, with that phrase 'smart casual' ringing in my ears. 'And possibly a hat', trilled my hostess over the phone. We were to meet at her home for a lunch party before heading for the river. It was a baking hot day and I was at my fattest. I put on a baggy white linen dress, which of course got creased in the car. We arrived in the town early and I caught a glimpse of myself in a shop window. I looked scruffy. I wailed to Richard that I'd have to stop to buy something to smarten me up. We shot into the first clothes shop we saw and emerged with a very pretty lace jacket that had cost me considerably more than I would normally spend. But when we finally arrived at the house I was confident I was definitely, in my terms at least, 'smart casual'. When our hostess opened the door I was amazed to see she was dressed in jeans, T-shirt and sandals with a very old looking sun hat in her hand. I was now obviously over-dressed.

I love that lace jacket and wear it all the time, but I've decided: when in doubt as to what to wear, always err on the side of understatement.

How to nurture your friends

Friendship is a living thing that, with a little nurturing, will flourish.

You should try to keep track of your friends' lives so

that when you next speak to them you can ask, for example, how a father's health is, whether a daughter is happy at her new school, or how that office row ended. And of course you will want to remember birthdays of special friends – a card or a call on the day is all it takes. I always make a note of the birthday in my diary the day before so that I *do* remember to send a card. And make sure you celebrate your friends' triumphs, however modest, by letting them know how pleased for them you are.

The day after a friend of mine chaired a highly successful panel discussion I sent her a short fax to congratulate her on her performance and all the effort I knew she'd put in behind the scenes to organise the event. She emailed me immediately: 'Thank you so much. You are a true friend'. I was so pleased.

There are so many quick, thirty-second ways you can keep in touch these days: email, postcard, text message or answer phone. But never leave a recorded message on the answer phone that is in any way less than friendly – you never know what mood your friend will be in when they eventually listen to it. If you're cross about something wait until you can speak to them directly.

Don't forget the importance of the 'thank you' note. I usually scribble something in my diary on the day after an event as a reminder. And in this age of computers and technology I think a 'thank you' note is one of the few things that you should definitely write by hand.

After a phone call or a lunch with a friend I sometimes jot down a reminder to ring a little later to follow up on anything important we've discussed – a driving test, a possible promotion at work, or a hospital check-up. And a telephone call for no reason at all except to keep in touch is a clear sign of your friendship. We all know those people who only ever ring when they want something from us – don't be one of them.

These brief contacts are such a good way of looking after friends – even if they say no more than 'Hi, thinking of you, hope we meet a little later in the year'. That's really why I send holiday postcards. I run off the addresses from my database before I go away and then I just have to stick the label on the card when I'm there. Of course when my friends get a card with a printed label they know that I've written to lots of people, but I hope they don't mind. At least it shows I've taken the trouble to look them up before I go and that I really do want to stay in touch.

The fact is I fret if I lose contact; that's why these little ways of keeping the current flowing through my network of friends are so essential to me.

Passing on your skills

Once you've begun to make friends and gained in confidence as a result, make it easy for others to learn your new skills. Encourage your friends to mix and circulate with each other. And if somebody new offers you a tentative hand of friendship, grab it. If a stranger looks lost at a party or at dinner – come to their rescue. Draw people to your side.

You are now the one who can help set the tone at a lunch, a business meeting or any other gathering. By introducing people to each other or starting the conversation, you can encourage networking.

Weddings are particularly difficult. Often nobody there knows anybody but the bride or the groom – and they are both understandably pre-occupied. So if you're a wedding guest offer a helping hand to anyone looking lost. Go over and start a conversation: 'Who is it you know, the bride or the groom?' is a good start.

Of course you mustn't force yourself and your socialising skills on other people at their do's, though I have to admit to my shame that these days I do sometimes find myself, without thinking, taking over a shy host's role. But there will be many occasions when you will be able to help transform something rather dull into a thoroughly enjoyable event.

Some people will say that spending so much time on friends and friendship is a distraction from the important business of developing yourself. But for me making friends and making the most of them – networking – doesn't mean that you lose your sense of being your own person. It doesn't mean you can't have days on your own to do things that are important only to you. It's just a matter of knowing that there *are* friends out there – friends who can make all the difference to your life, and you to theirs – if you take a little trouble to look after them.

Friendly Behaviour

Remember the 'friends etiquette': don't take advantage

When a friend in trouble doesn't respond, persevere – they'll be pleased later

If someone you've met through a friend has been helpful, let your friend know

Call your friends to find out how they're doing – for no other reason at all

Always return a call promptly – even if you intend to reply more fully later on

As you learn the art of making friends and networking, pass it on

14

Let's Rehearse!
getting it right

How does all this guidance in networking and the art of making friends actually work in practice? Soon, I hope, you'll be finding out. Meanwhile, here are some hypothetical scenarios to illustrate what I see as the do's and don't's of friendly behaviour.

I've sketched out six mini dramas to cover the sort of social or business occasions you might find yourself involved in. In each case my characters act either in a *friendly way* or an *unfriendly way*. For me, it highlights the very different outcomes as the curtain falls.

Sunday lunch

Sally is hosting Sunday lunch for eight friends – she's on her own. The table is laid, and she's decided where her guests will be sitting.

Friendly Way	Unfriendly Way
John is feeling awkward that he has arrived first. Sally tells him how helpful it would be if he would open some bottles and lay out some plates of eats.	John is feeling awkward that he has arrived first. Sally tells him that she's still getting things ready and will be out of the kitchen to talk to him in a moment.
The doorbell rings. Sally answers it herself, greets her next guest, Fiona, introduces her to John and gets him to pour her a drink.	The doorbell rings and Sally asks John to answer it. He doesn't know the guest, Fiona, who makes an awkward entrance. Sally gets distracted opening bottles. John and Fiona have to look after each other.

Fiona has brought a huge bouquet of flowers and a box of chocolates.
 	
    Sally exclaims with delight – says she looks forward to sampling a chocolate later and puts the box by her coffee tray. She then arranges
	Fiona has brought a huge bouquet of flowers and a box of chocolates.
	
	    Sally hardly acknowledges them. She waves vaguely towards the kitchen, asking John to find something to put the flowers in for the

Friendly Way	**Unfriendly Way**
the flowers quickly in a vase already filled with water that's close to hand.	time being. The chocolates lie unnoticed on the hall shelf.

The bell goes again. Sally excuses herself from her guests and opens the door. Partners Paul and Sue have arrived at the same time as Bob, whom they don't know. Sally quickly introduces them to each other as they enter. She's given two different bottles of wine, which she acknowledges with pleasure, but she says as the wine for lunch is already in the fridge, she will keep these for another day.

Sally introduces her new guests to John and Fiona, who have been chatting together for some time now. She gives her new arrivals a drink.

Sally looks at her watch; she's waiting for her last two guests. Knowing John and Fiona have been in conversation together for some time, she now decides

---

The bell goes again. Sally wants a private word with Fiona and asks John to let the new arrivals in. He opens the door to Paul, Sue and Bob, suggests they leave the wine they brought on the hall table, and waves them in the direction of the drawing room. They walk in looking rather lost, not knowing who Fiona is. By this time Sally has disappeared into the kitchen again. They wait some time in rather awkward conversation before Sally returns and offers them a drink.

Sally's lost the plot. She can't remember who she's waiting for and can't decide whether to keep the soup simmering or take it off the heat. She looks distracted.

167

Friendly Way	Unfriendly Way

not to sit them next to each other at lunch.

Sally has already prepared the cold starter (Parma ham and figs) and looks relaxed and ready to talk to her friends. She explains they are waiting for her last two guests and makes sure everyone's glass is filled.

Two people have an empty glass.

～

The bell rings again. Sally is there immediately to welcome Christine and Isabel. More flowers – again Sally has a vase filled with water near to hand.

She introduces her guests and gives them a drink. She puts the bread rolls in the warm oven and the starters on the table and tells everyone they'll be sitting down in about five minutes.

The bell rings again. John, without checking with Sally, goes to answer it. It's Christine and Isabel. John knows them and immediately starts chatting to them in the hall, ignoring the bouquet of flowers Isabel is holding. After two or three minutes they all wander into the room and nod in the direction of the other guests but go on talking amongst themselves. Sally does nothing to introduce them, but merely says 'hi' and suggests everyone sits down right away because the soup is nearly boiling. The bread rolls are cold; she's forgotten to put them in the oven.

Friendly Way	Unfriendly Way
Sally guides her guests to their places, and when all are seated, goes round the table to make sure everyone knows who they're sitting next to. She also makes sure everyone has a full glass, plus water if wanted, and then tells them to tuck in. She talks to Bob, sitting on her right, but keeps an eye open to make sure all her guests are engaged in conversation.	Sally lets everyone sit where they want to. John and Fiona look dismayed to end up sitting next to each other (they've almost run out of conversation), and on her other side Fiona is sitting next to someone she hasn't yet been introduced to. Sally serves the soup, plonks herself down, and then continually jumps up and down checking the cheese soufflé which is the main course. John asks if he can open another bottle of wine. Isabel asks for a glass of water – it's warm because Sally has forgotten to put the water in the fridge.
The first course finished, Sally asks Bob, at the seat nearest the kitchen, to help with the clearing. She tells everyone else to remain where they are. When Sally's served the main course (baked salmon, potatoes and salad) she introduces a topic of general interest to include	The first course finished, everyone stands up to help clear. The kitchen is in chaos. When Sally's finally served the main course (the soufflé) everyone carries on talking to their neighbour. One or two look a little left out of things, but Sally doesn't notice, so does nothing about it.

169

Friendly Way	Unfriendly Way

everybody in the same conversation.

Before Sally brings on the dessert, she suggests she swaps places with Christine, whom she has previously established won't mind, just to move her guests around a little. The cold pudding (lemon tart), prepared the day before, is superb.

Sally does nothing to help her guests start talking to other people. She's once again in the kitchen, trying to brown the pudding (crème brulée) under the grill. Conversation flags.

Sally moves her guests to the easy chairs for coffee, making sure they are now sitting next to someone different. She opens Fiona's chocolates, which she offers round. She remarks again on the flowers and wine she's been given.

Sally serves coffee to her guests, still seated at the table, still next to the same people. By now they're all pretty bored with their lunch companions but still haven't been introduced to all their fellow guests. Fiona's chocolates are forgotten.

The phone rings. Sally answers it in case it is a message for one of her guests, but when she finds it's for her, says immediately she is entertaining and will ring back later. She makes a

The phone rings. Sally answers it and disappears into the next room for a long conversation.

Friendly Way	Unfriendly Way

note on the phone pad to remind herself to do so.

~

Sally's lunch party breaks up after a couple of hours. Everyone has talked to everyone else and enjoyed the food and the conversation. They feel they've been warmly welcomed by Sally and well looked after.

Sally is delighted to see her guests swapping telephone numbers before they leave.

~

Sally's lunch party goes on too long, because she's had to do so much last-minute cooking. John makes his excuses and leaves before the coffee and the others gradually drift away, feeling a little neglected. They're disappointed they haven't been encouraged to talk to everyone there.

~

171

Party plan

Tom is hosting a mid-week party at his flat. He's told people not to expect food, but that drinks will be served between 6.00pm and 7.30pm. He's expecting about thirty of his friends. White wine and mineral water are in the fridge and glasses on a table in the entrance hall.

Friendly Way	**Unfriendly Way**
It's 5.55pm and Tom has just taken a couple of bottles of wine and one of water out of the fridge to the hall table. Five minutes later, on the dot of 6.00pm, the bell goes. Tom welcomes his first guests Paul and Mandy, and while they're signing the guest book (pen provided) he pours them a drink. They move through to chat in the main room.	It's 5.55pm and Tom is not yet ready for his guests. Five minutes later, on the dot of 6.00pm, the bell goes. Tom has still not opened a bottle of wine. He rushes to the door, looking flustered. Paul and Mandy say they hope they aren't too early. Tom asks them to sign the guest book, but there's no pen. He offers them a drink, but then has to rush to the kitchen to open a bottle, leaving Paul and Mandy on their own. He's only just got the cork out when …
The bell goes again. Tom excuses himself from his first guests, and opens the door to Yvonne, Laura and Tim.	The bell goes again. Tom hurries to the door, wine bottle in hand, to greet Yvonne, Laura and Tim. Tom

172

Friendly Way	Unfriendly Way
He asks them to sign the book and pours the wine and water they want just as the bell goes again. Tom quickly introduces his new guests to Paul and Mandy and then answers the door. It's his neighbour, Bill, and there's time to sign him in, give him a drink and introduce him to the others.	forgets to mention the guest book, and pours them each a glass of wine. But Laura wants water. Tom is about to get some when the bell goes once more. He asks Mandy to find the water, leaving his guests to introduce themselves to each other. He answers the door to his neighbour, Bill, gives him a drink and starts chatting to him.
The bell goes again. Tom's in the middle of a conversation, but politely excuses himself and answers the door. It's four of his sporting chums. He gets them to sign in, gives them a drink, and brings them in to the room to introduce them to the rest of his guests, explaining that they know each other through playing squash together.	The bell goes again. Tom is in the middle of a conversation in the main room and hopes someone else will answer the door. Laura finally opens it to four men she doesn't know. She tells them that Tom is in there somewhere. They go into the room without a drink and stay together in a huddle.
The bell goes. Tom answers. It's two attractive girls from work, Sue and Tania. Tom gives them a drink and then,	The bell goes. Tom answers. It's two attractive girls from work, Sue and Tania. He starts chatting to them in the

Friendly Way	Unfriendly Way

rather than trying to interrupt all the conversations around the room, introduces them to the nearest group, his squash friends. The bell goes – it's three more arrivals.

corridor, and by the time the bell goes again he still hasn't offered them a drink. He answers the door and now needs to find a drink for three more newcomers in addition to the two girls.

By 7.00pm most of Tom's guests have arrived. Tom has asked Tim to help make sure glasses are re-filled promptly, leaving him time to move guests around to make sure they meet as many different people as possible. He keeps a look out for anyone who seems lost or not engaged in a conversation.

By 7.00pm most of Tom's guests have arrived. Several people have empty glasses, and they can't find another bottle anywhere.

Two people have been talking to each other for half-an-hour and don't know how to escape. Another couple are stuck in the corner just looking on, having run out of conversation altogether.

Tom looks at the notes he's made to himself and remembers to give Mandy the Harry Potter book he'd promised her son.

It's 7.15pm. Tom attracts everyone's attention and thanks them for coming. He says 'If there's anyone here you'd like to meet and

It's 7.15pm. Tom's run out of wine.

Guests begin to drift away into the night …

Friendly Way	Unfriendly Way
haven't yet spoken to, then move around now while there's still time. If you're hungry there's a restaurant just around the corner that's usually got plenty of room.	
I'm going to have a bite to eat there later, let me know if you can join me.'	

~

Friendly Way	Unfriendly Way
It's 7.45pm. Most of Tom's guests have gone; they've met a lot of people and exchanged contact details. About half a dozen have gone ahead to the restaurant Tom recommended – he'll join them soon. Tom hastily scribbles a note to remind himself to ring Mandy in the morning as he's promised.	It's 7.45pm. Tom's guests have gone. Some of them only talked to people they knew already. Tom's trying to remember who asked him to call in the morning. His guest book, with few signatures, can't help him.

~

Friendly Way	Unfriendly Way
Before he goes to bed Tom looks at his guest book to remind himself of anything else he's promised to do for anyone.	Tom goes to bed and forgets everything he's been told or promised to do. The Harry Potter book is gathering dust.

~

An invitation to dinner

Sandra is a public relations executive. She's been invited to dinner with the boss of her advertising firm, Tony. It's on a Friday, a night her husband Peter usually likes to keep free for relaxing at the end of the week, but Sandra's persuaded him to come too. 'Nothing formal', she's been told, just ten for dinner, including the personnel director from work (whom she doesn't get on with very well). They've been asked to arrive between 8pm and 8.15pm.

Friendly Way	Unfriendly Way
7.30pm Peter's looking grumpy. He doesn't want to go to the dinner and is taking his time dressing. Sandra wants them to be in harmony at the dinner. She gives Peter a big hug, says she understands how he feels but tells him that his support means a lot to her. Peter grins and quickly finishes dressing. Sandra reminds herself this evening is a chance not only to get to know Tony but also to make one or two new friends and maybe even get on good terms with the personnel director. They leave.	7.30pm Peter's looking grumpy. He doesn't want to go to the dinner and is taking his time dressing. Sandra fumes and tells him to hurry up, it's time to go. She's feeling worried about meeting the personnel director. They leave late, in frosty silence.

Friendly Way	Unfriendly Way
8.05pm Sandra and Peter arrive in good time. Tony introduces them to his wife Rita and his other guests. Sandra spots the personnel director, gives him a broad smile and begins chatting to his wife, whom she's never met. They get on well.	8.25pm Sandra and Peter arrive late. Tony introduces them to his wife Rita and his other guests and says they're about to sit down for dinner. Sandra glares at the personnel director and ignores his wife.

~

At the table Sandra is sitting between a GP and Tony's accountant. She spends time over the first course finding out how the GP runs his surgery, what he thinks about the latest NHS deals. Over the main course she turns to the accountant and asks him how he keeps so many figures in his head and what's the most difficult part of his job. She looks across at Peter who smiles – he's doing his best to get on well with their hostess Rita.	At the table Sandra is sitting between a GP and Tony's accountant. She spends time over the first course asking the GP what she should do about her hay fever and Peter's lack of energy. Over the main course she continues to talk to the GP and ignores the accountant, thinking he'll be dull. She looks across to Peter whom she hears laying down the law about the City to the personnel director. (Peter knows nothing about the City and he's talking straight across Rita, ignoring her.)

~

177

Friendly Way	Unfriendly Way
Before the pudding the hosts swap people around. Sandra stays next to the GP but has a new man on her right. He begins a conversation with his other neighbour, leaving Sandra with no-one to talk to. She leaves it for a few minutes, then leans towards the man until he realises she's been left out and includes her in what he's saying. They have a good discussion about a film they've all seen.	Before the pudding the hosts swap people around. Sandra stays next to the GP but has a new man on her right. He begins a conversation with his other neighbour, leaving Sandra with no-one to talk to. She sulks, stares woodenly ahead and feels her colour rising. After a few minutes she goes to the loo and has a cigarette. When she returns she finds everyone has moved into the drawing room for coffee.

Friendly Way	Unfriendly Way
It's coffee in easy chairs. Sandra feels snubbed that Tony has made no effort to talk to her but decides to give him the benefit of the doubt – it could just be because he's distracted. She goes over to him and says how much she is enjoying the evening. He beams, says he's sorry he hasn't had a chance to chat, and they establish a real rapport. The personnel director comes over and joins in the conversation, returning	It's coffee in easy chairs. Sandra feels snubbed that Tony hasn't sought her out, and she makes no effort to talk to anyone herself. Across the room Peter looks fed up and keeps pointing rather obviously at his watch. He wants to leave. Sandra refuses to take the hint. They stay another half-an-hour without contributing anything.

Friendly Way	Unfriendly Way
Sandra's smile. Across the room Peter looks happy enough, but makes a sign he's ready to go home when she is. They leave shortly afterwards.	

~

| It's midnight. Sandra tells Peter she was pleased to talk to her boss Tony. She also feels she's established a good relationship with the personnel director and his wife; perhaps they could invite them to a buffet lunch one Sunday – of course including Tony and Rita. Peter says that sounds fine. Sandra says how pleased she was Peter gave up his evening to come with her; she'll bring him a cup of tea in bed. Peter feels pleased his support was appreciated. | 12.30am Sandra is tired and cross with herself that she didn't go over and talk to Tony. Peter's had too much to drink and vaguely realises he was too strident when talking to the personnel director. He tells Sandra he knew he shouldn't have come. He's off to bed, will she please turn out the lights. |

~

Evening drinks

Norma and her boyfriend Greg have been invited by Pauline, who works for a fashion buyer, to drinks at her home. 6.00pm to 7.30pm, 'smart casual', they're told.

Friendly Way	Unfriendly Way
6.15pm Norma and Greg arrive at Pauline's home. Norma is wearing an understated silk shirt and tailored skirt and smart but comfortable shoes. She has a small bag slung over her shoulder. Greg wears a stylish shirt and casual suit. (He has his tie in his pocket in case everyone's wearing one – but they're not.)	6.45pm Norma and Greg arrive at Pauline's home. Norma is wearing her highest heels and a glittering cocktail dress which is a bit too tight on the hips. She has to keep tugging it down. She's brought her big satchel bag from the office and has to plonk it in the bedroom when she arrives – it's too heavy to keep with her. Greg has stubbornly dressed right down – he's wearing a T-shirt.
Pauline introduces her guests to a small group already in conversation and moves on. Norma and Greg join in for a few minutes before Norma says she just wants to say hello to so and so, and tells Greg she'll see him a little later. Greg knows	Pauline introduces her guests to a small group already in conversation and moves on. Norma and Greg join in and stay for twenty minutes. Norma's not sure how to leave the group. Eventually it breaks up and Norma and Greg talk to

Friendly Way	Unfriendly Way

Norma prefers to work a room alone and stays happily chatting to the others. Norma joins a new group, says: 'Hello I'm Norma, I know Pauline through our mutual friend Susan.' After about five minutes, she leaves that group saying she wants to find a glass of water, and then starts chatting to another woman on her own. When she wants to move on she attracts the attention of a friend whom she introduces to the woman she's with, before saying she must go and talk to someone before they leave.

themselves for ten minutes, not sure how to get into conversation with anyone else. Greg is feeling restless. A woman joins them, but after a while Norma is bored, makes their excuses and drags Greg off to refresh their drinks, leaving the woman standing on her own.

~

Norma now has three people whose names she wants to remember. She discreetly pulls out the pen and paper in her bag, jots down their names and continues to circulate, waiting on the edge of a group for the right moment before introducing herself. She meets a woman she already knows slightly

Norma has only met one other person whose name she wants to remember, but with no pen and paper to hand she can't write it down, and she has no card of her own to hand to anyone else. Frustrated, she drags Greg over to two people in earnest conversation, and barges in without a thought.

Friendly Way	Unfriendly Way
and, after a friendly chat, hands over her business card, saying she'll call her later in the week.	They look irritated – obviously in the middle of an important chat. Norma doesn't notice.
7.20pm Norma and Greg meet up again, say their goodbyes to Pauline and go to the nearby restaurant they've previously booked. They've had a good evening and made two or three new contacts – potential friends.	7.50pm Norma and Greg are amongst the last to leave. They spend twenty minutes trying to find a restaurant with a table that's free, give up and go home.
10pm They're home. Norma puts the names of those she's met in her address book, with a note to ring one of them within the next few days. She writes a quick thank you note to Pauline on behalf of Greg and herself.	8.30pm They're home. Norma's cross she can't remember the name of the person she wanted to ring. Greg's cross too. He feels they out-stayed their welcome – and he's hungry. Neither gets around to writing a thank you note.

The business lunch

Tim, a public affairs consultant, has been invited to a business lunch. The host is Ken, the Director of Corporate Affairs for a public utility company. The discussion will be about public and private enterprise. The venue is a trendy members' club in central London. There will be twelve people – he's already received a list of the guests. 12.45pm for 1pm.

Friendly Way	Unfriendly Way
12.50pm Tim arrives and is introduced to the others. He looks at his guest list and makes a mental note of who's who – three or four he knows already. He's checked up through colleagues on one or two others and even went as far as asking Ken's PA for their CV's. Now he introduces himself to them for a chat before lunch.	1.10pm Tim arrives rather late and is introduced to the others. But he's forgotten his guest list and is muddled about who's who. He already knows three or four of those there and heads in their direction, but almost at once Ken announces lunch.
1.15pm Ken suggests everyone finds their place card and sits down. Then after a few minutes he introduces the topic for discussion and asks the most senior guest to kick off. When two or three have spoken Tim makes a couple of salient points – he's done his	1.15pm Ken suggests everyone finds their place card and sits down. Then after a few minutes he introduces the topic for discussion and asks the most senior guest to kick off. Tim is horrified to realise he will be expected to say something. He hasn't

183

Friendly Way	Unfriendly Way
homework on both the subject and the various companies represented around the table, so feels fairly confident. He has his guest list in front of him and has worked out who's sitting where.	brushed up on the subject and knows nothing about two of the companies represented. And he's forgotten who's who around the table. After half-an-hour Ken asks Tim what he wants to say. Tim lamely repeats a point that's already been made and then peters out…
2.15pm Ken rounds off the discussion and invites his guests to mingle for the last 15 minutes. Tim joins the two people he hasn't yet spoken to and makes a note on his guest list of one or two telephone numbers and things he wants to follow up. Then he seeks out Ken, thanks him and leaves. Tim kept to just one glass of wine as he has a meeting later that afternoon.	2.15pm Ken rounds off the discussion and invites his guests to mingle for the last 15 minutes. Tim, realising he's not made a success of the lunch, sees this as his chance to escape. While Ken is busy talking to someone else, Tim leaves without saying goodbye to him. He has not made a single note and realizes he's wasted an opportunity. In his anxiety he's also had three glasses of wine and feels muddle-headed for his next meeting.

Friendly Way	Unfriendly Way
Next day he rings the person he promised to contact and fixes a meeting with what is now a potential client.	Next day he forgets to ring the person he promised to contact. A potential client has been lost.

Coffee morning

Linda is holding a coffee morning at her home on a Wednesday. She's asked about a dozen people to call in if they can, and bring a friend if they wish. Eight have said they will definitely be there some time between 10am and 11.30am.

Friendly Way	Unfriendly Way
10.10am No-one has arrived. Linda makes sure the coffee is in the pot, the milk warming and the biscuits on the table. She has a dozen cups ready just in case they all turn up. She relaxes, looking forward to her guests arriving.	10.10am No-one has arrived. Linda decides to wait until someone is there before brewing the coffee. She hopes she has enough milk. There aren't many biscuits, but she has some croissants to heat up if necessary. She has eight cups set out.
10.15am The first guest arrives with another friend Linda doesn't know. She welcomes them both. She pours coffee, offers biscuits and learns a little about the newcomer.	10.15am The first guest arrives with another friend Linda doesn't know. Linda leaves them to talk to each other while she goes to make the coffee.
The bell goes and Linda's good friend Gwen arrives. Linda again offers coffee and biscuits and introduces her guests to each other.	The bell goes and Linda's good friend Gwen arrives. Linda asks Gwen to come and help her in the kitchen. They stand there chatting,

Friendly Way	Unfriendly Way
	ignoring the two guests waiting for their coffee.
	~
~	
Two guests who don't know each other arrive together. Linda gives them coffee and introduces them to the others with a suitable one liner: 'Mary I know from my yoga evening class, and Sue is the star of the local dramatic society.' Sue asks for herb tea instead of coffee – Linda can offer peppermint or camomile.	Two guests who don't know each other arrive together. Linda has at last made the coffee. She hurriedly introduces everyone by name, but doesn't tell them anything about each other. Sue asks for herb tea instead of coffee – Linda doesn't have any. Milk and biscuits are both running out. Linda's getting flustered trying to heat up the croissants. She has no time to concentrate on her guests, and make sure they network.
	~
~	
11.15am There are now ten guests.	11.15am There are now ten guests. Linda is flagging. She sits down and chats exclusively to her friend Gwen.
Linda moves around everyone, making sure they're all engaged in conversation. She mentions a movie she wants to see and asks if anyone else fancies seeing it too. Three say yes, and one offers to sort out a date.	She forgets to remind her guests as they leave that she will be holding another coffee morning at her home, same time, same day of the week, a month from now –

187

Friendly Way	Unfriendly Way
Linda says she's been planning to turn out her cupboards for a car boot sale – two of her friends say they want to do the same. Linda promises to ring them later. As people leave, Linda says she'll be holding another coffee morning at her home, same time, same day of the week, a month from now. She asks her guests to ring her if they can make it and let her know if they wish to bring a friend.	she'll have to ring them all to let them know. More work, she thinks. Is it worth it?
12 noon. Everyone has left. Linda feels satisfied. She makes a note to remind her two friends about the car boot sale.	12 noon. Everyone has left. Linda is exhausted. She's got nothing new or satisfying out of this morning. Only now does she remember she meant to suggest a car boot sale and mention a film she wants to see. She'd hoped to find someone to do these things with.

Epilogue

Writing this book has made me re-examine my own feel-ings about my friends: why am I still spending so many hours of my life trying to meet more people and keep track of every one of them? Is it really necessary?

After all, I could probably carry on my work and earn a living for years ahead without having to meet anyone new – apart from those I naturally bump into in the course of my daily business. I could let my membership of all those think tanks and networking groups lapse, yet still have plenty of places where I could see my existing friends and colleagues. I need never hold another huge Christmas party or regular salon. Instead I could just continue to entertain on a much smaller scale at home.

I know my darling mother would have been happy for me to cut back. Years ago now she urged me to stop my annual party, because she thought it was too much hard work: 'It's a millstone around your neck, dear,' she said.

So why do I feel so strongly that I have to carry on putting people together? Why am I so driven to see that they network successfully with each other?

I think it's this. If I am obsessed with meeting people and making friends with them – and I am – it's because I've gained so much from it. Just as people helped me to overcome my shyness when I set out in life, so today I feel compelled to encourage other people in the same way. I can remember now the pure pleasure I felt if anyone included me in something they were organising with their friends. And I can equally well remember my disappointment when people promised to invite me to a social occasion or introduce me to someone they knew – and then didn't do it. That's why I'm so insistent in this book on delivering what you promise.

Making friends is wonderful; helping other people make them has proved more satisfying still. I've become hooked on the excitement of putting together people from very different worlds and seeing them grow as they begin to benefit from each other's company. So I hope this book encourages you to be open to new friendships and then to go on to bring people together yourself. I see it as a sort of 'warm hug' to reassure you that learning the art of making friends really can enrich your life.

I would love to think that there will be a real revival of the salon – that everywhere people will start a regular get-together at a set time, on a set day, in a set venue to meet their friends and potential friends in whatever way suits them best.

But there's no need at all to become as caught up in all this as I am – forever adding more people to my database – in order to make friends and make the most of them.

I'll be happy if you can go along with me as far as this: discovering just as I did that friends are the joy of life, the demonstration that we're not alone in this world.

My mother may have thought my parties were hard work for me – and she was right – yet she loved to be there. I can see her now, wandering from group to group with her quiet smile, eyes shining. She'd hold out her hand and say: 'Hello, I'm Kathleen, I'm Carole's mother.'

Mama put no pressure on me to succeed, yet I knew she felt I could do anything at all if I really wanted to. 'Sweetheart', she'd say to me: 'take life by the scruff of the neck; know that somehow you'll cope whatever comes your way.' Mama wanted me to fulfil my potential and not be afraid of failure. She was my inspiration in life as she is in her death.

My mother encouraged me to be interested in other people and to hold out my hand in friendship. I hope this book will encourage you to do the same: 'Hello, I'm Carole Stone …'

Carole's Six Commitments

No matter the situation, always be ready to
make a friend

The best way to make a friend is to
be interested in other people

Don't be possessive – share your friends
with other friends

Keep your friendships in good repair –
nurture your network

Accept your friends for what they are –
nobody's perfect

Network your friends – and watch
them benefit